Prospects for Human Survival

Second Edition

by

Willard H. Wells

To Chuck

Willard

Published by Lifeboat Foundation
lifeboat.com

ISBN-13: 978-0998413105
ISBN-10: 0998413100
Cover by J. Daniel Batt

PRINTED IN THE UNITED STATES OF AMERICA

OTHER BOOKS BY LIFEBOAT FOUNDATION

The Human Race to the Future: What Could Happen—and What to Do
by Daniel Berleant

Visions of the Future
Edited by J. Daniel Batt

Learn more at lifeboat.com/ex/books.

To my progeny and my readers:
May you and your loved ones
survive the apocalypse.

Revised Preface to First Edition

This book is an update of my previous book *Apocalypse When?*. Both versions use a mathematical formulation that reduces the complex topic of human survivability to the simple mathematical formula that appears on the cover of this book. This reduction is quite unusual; its justification appears in Chapter 4 supported by several appendixes.

Readers whose math skills are impaired by lack of practice, especially second-year algebra and precalculus, may be reassured by a list of professionals who have vetted this formulation. I am aware of eight, seven of whom approve, only one objects. They are the following:

- John J. Watkins, Dept. Mathematics & Computer Science, Colorado College, Colorado Springs, CO. He is the author of an editorial book review that appears in *The Mathematical Intelligencer*, Vol. 34, pp 71-2. "I for one am satisfied that Wells has built up a sufficient 'preponderance of evidence' that requires his final conclusions to be taken seriously."
- Stephen Webb, Ph.D. theoretical physics, lecturer, Open University, England. Dr. Webb was subject advisory editor of *Apocalypse When?*.
- Larry Carter, Professor Emeritus of Computer Science & Engineering, U. Cal. at San Diego (UCSD). Dr. Carter organized my public

lecture on the UCSD campus, on Oct. 15, 2009.

- S. Gill Williamson, Professor Emeritus of math, U. Cal. San Diego. He reviewed *Apocalypse When?* on Amazon.com.
- James Blodgett holds a MS degree in statistics. He is Coordinator of the Global Risk Reduction Special Interest Group in American Mensa.
- Ted Weverka, Ph.D. electrical engineering, Licensing mgr, engineering & physical sciences, U. Colorado. He reviewed *Apocalypse When?* on Amazon.com.
- Richard Puetter, Ph.D. physics, UCSD, Research Physicist, UCSD. Rick was a reviewer of an early version prior to publication.
- Samuel Goldberg, Professor Emeritus of math, Oberlin College, Ohio. Dr. Goldberg wrote the only unfavorable editorial review of *Apocalypse When?*. He is not persuaded that the assumptions substantiate the mathematics as he states in *The College Mathematics Journal*, Vol. 42, pp. 413–15, Nov. 2011. I have not asked him to read this update as he is now 92 years old.

Besides the reviewers listed above, I owe special thanks to Dr. Henri Hodara. He introduced me to this subject by way of J. Richard Gott's predictions and then encouraged me as I expanded on Gott's ideas. Special thanks to Eric Klien whose diligent editing resulted in many corrections and improvements.

Preface to Second Edition

This book differs from my first book *Apocalypse When?* primarily by including threats from digital technology. In particular, the worm Stuxnet proved that smart destructive software can usurp the hardware it needs to cause physical damage. The threat of digital tech also includes artificial intelligence, AI, the machine of the future that many fear will outsmart its human masters and impose some unknown will of its own.

I give small statistical weight to digital tech because it applies only in specialized high-tech areas, not quotidian matters in our daily lives. Nevertheless, its effect is disproportionately great because it has been increasing exponentially for the past fifty years at an extraordinary pace. According to the so-called Moore's Law, it doubles about every two years. (Over fifty years, that comes to a factor of 34 million.) Two early critiques of the first edition persuaded me that I should make this statistical weight even smaller. In particular, James Blodgett reminded me that every exponential process eventually hits a physical limit that ends its wild ride, and Moore's Law in particular may be due to stop. Accordingly, the main change in this edition is reduced hazards from digital tech.

I have also revised the graph for survivability of the human race, actually inverted it to probability of extinction. Previously it gave an average over various uncertain parameters, which was relatively easy to compute. However, averages can be misleading due to extreme outliers. I have now acquired more powerful mathematical software, Maple 2016, that allowed me to convert to more meaningful statistics such as the median.

Some people react adversely to the very idea of calculating human survivability. For example, I am a member of San Diego Independent Scholars (SDIS). Whenever a member publishes a book, they donate a copy to the library at the local university. I watched for *Apocalypse When?* to appear in the library's online book catalog. When it did not, I inquired and eventually received an email message from a librarian stating that they had rejected it and added it to their rummage sale of surplus books, even though it was published by Springer, a world-class science publisher. I reported this to the board of SDIS, who may have changed their policy.

Normally when an SDIS member publishes a book, (s)he is invited to make a presentation at a monthly meeting, but no invitation was forthcoming. A few inquiries revealed that the program chairman was dead set against it. Eventually a subgroup called Works in Progress invited me to speak. The program chairman attended and told me to my face that she was opposed to such obvious nonsense. Others looked at her in disbelief. Soon an opening occurred in the schedule, the board overruled the program chairman, and I was invited to speak. My lecture was apparently well received.

Helpful criticism says something specific, such as, 'I don't see how Equation 7 follows from your third assumption.' Such critiques, like the one from Blodgett, are rare. Vague unsupported rejection is much more common.

Read updates and revisions to this book at
https://lifeboat.com/ex/survivability

TABLE OF CONTENTS

TABLE OF FIGURES

TABLE OF PICTURES

Prospects for Human Survival

by Willard H. Wells

For what it's worth, our ancestor *Homo erectus* lasted about 15,000 centuries, and our cousins the Neanderthal lasted 2,000 cnt. We have also lasted 2,000 cnt and counting. They were subjected only to natural hazards, nothing of their own creation. They were more vulnerable than we since they had neither means for forecasting hazards, nor transportation for rapid escape. This suggests that our prospects against natural threats are quite good as shown mathematically below. Our big hazards are dangerous artifacts, everything from nuclear weapons to artificial microbes. Since there is no evidence that Erectus & Neanderthal made such things, further comparison is not useful.

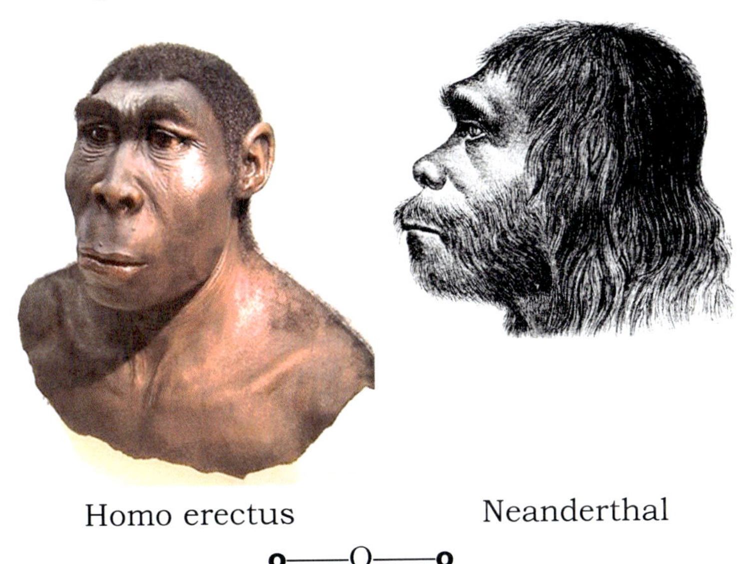

Homo erectus Neanderthal

o——O——o

Martin Rees is Britain's Astronomer Royal, past president of the Royal Socicty, and former master of Trinity College. He thinks that our civilization has about an even chance of surviving for 100 years.[1] Rees has also wagered $1,000 that a single incident of bio-error or bio-terror will kill a million people prior to 2020.

Stephen Hawking, the renowned astrophysicist, has stated, "We are entering an increasingly dangerous period of our history. Our population and our use of the finite resources of planet Earth are growing exponentially, along with our technical ability to change the environment for good or ill. But our genetic code still carries the selfish and aggressive instincts that were of survival advantage in the past. It will be difficult enough to avoid disaster in the next hundred years, let alone the next thousand or million. Our only chance of long-term survival is not to remain lurking on planet Earth, but to spread out into space."[2] Citing, in particular, the threat of new biological weapons, Hawking also said, "I don't think the human race will survive the next thousand years, unless we spread into space. There are too many accidents that can befall life on a single planet."

John Derbyshire has written *We Are Doomed: Reclaiming Conservative Pessimism,*[3] a screed against many trends in Western Civilization and the United States in particular. One is tempted to ignore a screed, except that Derbyshire has an intellect that must be taken seriously. I am acquainted with him through his previous book, *Prime Obsession: Bernhard Riemann and the Greatest Unsolved Problem in Mathematics.*[4] Derbyshire treats the weird properties of Riemann's zeta function making them accessible to all but hard-core mathphobes.

In *We Are Doomed* Derbyshire's writing is erudite with each point carefully reasoned and supported by evidence. He makes blunt statements with no concession to political rectitude. He argues that we have passed the point of no return and that the chance of recovery is exceedingly small. In particular, he notes the power of differential birth rates by which Islam will conquer Europe, while America will have more time.

At the end of his treatise, Derbyshire remarks on his great good luck to be born at the end of World War II, a time of peaceful progress. Then he concludes with a poignant message to his children: "I am sorry to have brought you into this mess. ... Even ... people like your dad ... live in part by brute biological instinct, and there is no instinct stronger than the one to [procreate]. So here you are." Another commentator might compartmentalize his thinking, family and business, but Derbyshire is too disciplined to lapse into the palliative of denial. He knows there is only one world, and his family is embedded in it.

John Leslie,[5] a Canadian philosopher, thinks humanity will survive another five centuries with about 70% confidence. After that we will either be extinct or will have spread to habitats beyond Earth per Hawking's recommendation. If at least one colony is completely weaned from Earth, then we will be virtually immune from extinction. Redundancy is security: if life on Earth dies, we still have a human colony elsewhere, and vice versa. The few centuries from now till then are a crucial time; afterward we shall be safe again.

Many other scholars have grown increasingly uneasy about humanity's survival prospects. Global warming is a major concern,[6] also the accelerating pace at which powerful man-made hazards are appearing and thriving, faster than mere mortals can adequately analyze the risks and adapt to them with the safety of former times. Examples are engineered viruses, nanotechnology, artificial intelligence, and much more. This treatise is not a plea to build in extra supervision, warnings and safeguards. These precautions work up to a point of diminishing returns, and beyond that they merely add complexity, itself a major cause of disaster.[7]

All this concern is reflected in a spate of a dozen books on human survival that appeared from 1996 to 2013.[8] Perhaps the most comprehensive is *Global Catastrophic Risks* by Bostrom and Ćirković,[9] which has 22 chapters by 25 authors. Philosopher Bostrom is director of the Future of Humanity Institute at Oxford University. He regards as "catastrophic" those hazards that threaten the human race with extinction, greatly reduce its potential, or cause the collapse of civilization. Folks who like fancy words call this "existential risk."

My previous book on human survivability is *Apocalypse When?* (Springer 2009).[10] I shall refer to it many times by its initials *AW*. It is unique in that it gives a top-down analysis of survivability culminating in a mathematical formula for survival probability. Although *AW* discusses specific hazards to human survival, the formula does not refer to them in any way. Instead, it depends on a ratio of humanity's future risk exposure to its past exposure. The past exposure is a measure of our proven robustness, while our future exposure (to any specified date in question) represents future jeopardy that we may or may not survive. Exposure, in turn, is represented by a composite of statistical quantities that indicate accelerating human activity, especially hazardous high tech activity.

This separation between survival formulas and a list of hazards is important because the main global catastrophic risks a few decades from now are unforeseeable. An article in The Atlantic[11] magazine explains:

> "[N]early all of the most threatening global catastrophic risks were unforeseeable a few decades before they became apparent. Forty years before the discovery of the nuclear bomb, few could have predicted that nuclear weapons would come to be one of the leading global catastrophic risks. Immediately after the Second World War, few could have known that catastrophic climate change, biotechnology, and artificial intelligence would come to pose such a significant threat."

My original formula expressed the probability of survival as a product of two factors. The first represented natural hazards, whose risk rate is constant; the probability of an asteroid strike during one century is much the same as any other century. The second factor represented man-made hazards whose risk rate accelerates at a pace typical of human activity as measured by various statistical indicators such as gross world product and the rate of publishing papers in science and engineering. These two factors have fractional exponents that total 1.0. These exponents are statistical weights that represent the relative number of ways the two categories of disaster can happen.

I could have included a third factor for risks that accelerate at the exponential pace of digital technology, Moore's law and similar indicators.[12] However, at that time, 2008, this technology did not seem to be a global threat. Well, one could imagine robots programmed to be hostile. They can surely kill many people before we kill them, but this is hardly a global threat. In any case, I did not include this third factor in my original formula for survivability.

This was a mistake. A year after publication of *AW*, the computer worm Stuxnet[13] appeared and demonstrated that sophisticated software can hijack the weapons it needs to wreak havoc! And Stuxnet is only the beginning, a very sophisticated program written by humans; it was not written by superhuman artificial intelligence (AI), which will bring far more serious hazards in years to come. AI may evolve into an all-powerful super-intelligence, which like Stuxnet can commandeer whatever weapons it needs to enforce its authority. Sorry if this seems like science fiction, but these are the kinds of hazards we may face as modern technology surges toward the so-called "Singularity." Consequently, my revision here includes all three factors: natural and man-made hazards as before, plus digital tech. The statistical weight of digital tech (number of ways it can happen) is very small because it occurs only in special high-tech scenarios, not commonplace badness such as terrorism, polluted rivers, corrupt officials or simple neglect. However, even with its puny statistical weight the factor has major impact due to its exponential increase.

My original results that appear in *AW* are reasonably consistent with the survival estimates by Martin Rees and John Leslie mentioned above. However, my current revision is not; the new estimate is much greater, and the half-life of our civilization drops to only a few decades. The risk rate for civilization's collapse is about 4.5% per year, which exceeds the risk of ordinary perils that insurance companies underwrite. This is truly frightening! A cataclysm that causes the collapse of civilization will kill billions including some of your friends and family as well as mine. Obviously, something **must** intervene in some way that nullifies the world model on which my calculation is based.

So what can we do? As a U.S. citizen I can urge my elected representatives to pass laws that halt research, relinquish new technology, slow the economy, and so on. But this is futile, it would make me a luddite, a dirty word in this country. The whole concept is un-American. Besides, I cannot persuade a significant number of senators and congressmen to read my documentation, essentially Chapter 4 below. My formulation is mathematical, and a majority of them are incapable of understanding it. Besides, even if the U.S. did renounce modern progress, other nations would happily step into the breach and maintain the threats to civilization. Perhaps an intervention that saves civilization will have to be so powerful that it undermines democratic governance.

Can you propose **any** worldwide intervention (short of World War III) that has any chance of success? If so, tell me, tell the Lifeboat Foundation, tell the world! Only one untried possibility may have the requisite power, artificial intelligence. We need a friendly AI overlord programmed to protect humanity from itself. But the drawback is that it may not be as friendly to humans as we hope. Then again the overlord may find and destroy a clandestine evil AI programmed by terrorists. We face a very uncertain future!

James Blodgett explained the concept to an email group. James is Coordinator of the Global Risk Reduction Special Interest Group in American Mensa. He wrote ...

> [My] parable posits a sleepy island village with a small airfield, serviced by a weekly passenger flight. The last plane blew one of several tires on landing, so there is a 1% chance the entire landing gear will blow on its next use. This is much too high odds for passenger flight, so the plane is parked on the tarmac awaiting a replacement tire. Meanwhile the island volcano erupts, and a flood of lava is headed toward the village. So everyone jumps on the plane and takes off.
>
> If Willard [yours truly] is right, it turns the precautionary principle on its head. It may be a reason to justify risky measures that have some probability of solving the problem. For example, it might be a reason to push forward on AI research despite incomplete safety measures, and hope to develop a friendly version, and hope that it can ... take over the world in a friendly way and save us from ourselves. ...
>
> Solutions cost money as well as risk. Willard's results might justify spending more money on possible solutions. If Willard is right, his results should be on the intellectual agenda. Also, we should vet his results [Chapter 4 below] to see if there is some way he might be wrong.

We might sell the concept of an AI overlord to AI gurus many of whom are fully able to understand and appreciate my analysis in Chapter 4. More likely, they will not be aware of my analysis, but will realize the need on their own. They in turn may not try to sell the concept to the U.S. Congress or anyone else in authority, who would be unable to understand my analysis or theirs. These gurus may just create the overlord and let it blindside everybody. No nation now forbids research in AI. If and when they do, there is always another nation that will allow it, especially if members of their leader's family are put on the payroll.

One such guru, Dr. Ben Goertzel,[14] already advocates an AI caretaker, which he calls AI Nanny.[15]

> The Singularity, or something like it, is probably near, and the outcome is radically uncertain in almost every way. How can we, as a culture and a species, deal with this situation? One possible solution is to build a powerful yet limited AGI (Artificial General Intelligence) system, with the explicit goal of keeping things on the planet under control while we figure out the hard problem of how to create a probably positive Singularity. That is: to create an "AI Nanny."
>
> The AI Nanny would forestall a full-on Singularity for a while, restraining it into what Max More has called a Surge, and giving us time to figure out what kind of Singularity we really want to build and how. It's not entirely clear that creating such an AI Nanny is plausible, but I've come to the conclusion it probably is. Whether or not we should try to create it—that is the Zillion-Dollar Question.

Until someone finds another intervention that nullifies my analysis in Chapter 4, the answer to Goertzel's "Zillion-Dollar Question" is a resounding YES because the risk without it is unequivocally unacceptable.

My new estimate of the half-life of civilization falls in the range 18 to 51 years. What does it mean to quote a range of half-life? Ordinarily an unstable system (such as a radioactive atom) has exactly one half-life. Given a statistical sample of such systems, the half-life is simply the time in which half of them die off. If we had survival statistics for hundreds of expired humanoid species on Earth-like planets throughout the galaxy, then we could indeed derive one value of half-life. But these data are not available, and so we are stuck using probability theory to estimate the unknown half life, which then gives a range. In other words we shall impose a sort of metaprobability on top of ordinary probability theory.

In his article Dr. Goertzel writes, "I think we could have [an AI Nanny] in a couple decades if we really put our collective minds to it." Goertzel's 20 years compares to my half-life range 18 to 51 years. No time to lose!

If you are a philanthropist eager to support research, you need not wait to investigate the most daunting questions: What is artificial consciousness? Artificial emotion? You can fund a project that is peripheral to the big questions, but essential nonetheless. For example, robots do not yet have full mammalian vision. Sophisticated robots should routinely look at stereo images of a scene and make a list of objects along with coordinates of each one: a tree, a chair, a man, a child, a package, a fence. Many robots sense objects as obstacles they must avoid, but without complete identification and mapping.

Or maybe you can sponsor a contest to find the next AI genius, somebody like Alan Turing of Bletchley Park or Larry Page and Sergey Brin of Google. She may be milking cows in Moldova. Wherever, find her! My point is, we need to start now.

Back to Dr. Goertzel's article. He favors some sort of international democratic cooperation in setting up the AI Nanny. I am skeptical of that, hence the verb *blindside* in my discussion above. When Goertzel wrote his article in 2011 he did not have my figures showing the urgency of the project. He may have assumed it can wait until a favorable period of international cooperation, during which it can be sold to authorities in a normal democratic manner.

Finally, Goertzel concludes his article with a list of objections that people have raised. The final one is, “But it’s odious!!”, to which he replies,

> Yes, it’s odious. Government is odious too, but apparently necessary. And as Winston Churchill said, “democracy is the worst form of government except all those other forms that have been tried.” ... I wouldn’t have written this article when I was 22, because back then I was more steadfastly oriented toward idealistic solutions, but now, at age 44, I’ve pretty well come to terms with the universe’s persistent refusal to behave in accordance with all my ideals. The AI Nanny scenario is odious in some respects, but can you show me an alternative that’s less odious and still at least moderately realistic? I’m all ears....

o—O—o

Before slogging through the abstractions in my mathematical formulation, readers may wish to review global catastrophic risks and acquire some intuition for their severity and what hope we have to survive them. Accordingly, Chapter 1 bears the title “Artificial Intelligence, Chapter 2 “Other threats to humankind,” and Chapter 3 “How to save the human race.” Then Chapter 4 gives the “Numerical estimates of survivability.” As mentioned above, the analysis in Chapter 4 depends only on categories of hazards in a very general way. Thus it is remarkably independent of specific hazards discussed in Chapters 1 & 2. In fact, this analysis would remain valid even if my assessment of specific hazards were entirely invalid.

You may read Chapters 1 to 4 in any sequence. A final Chapter 5 offers a few pages of advice.

Chapter 1. Artificial intelligence

Computers already far exceed human capability in specialized tasks such as arithmetic, copying and searching files, and so on. But here we consider an artificial intelligence (AI) that does everything the human mind can do and more, which is sometimes called "artificial general intelligence." Eventually AI is expected to surpass human intelligence. Many experts expect this momentous event to happen sometime in the latter half of this century.

Human programmers cannot completely control the development of this super intelligence since they do not know how to directly write code for the human brain, much less anything superior. But they can write code that initiates an evolutionary process whereby their computer writes its own AI code. This is a recursive process in which each generation of AI produces a new generation having greater intelligence. Each iteration makes changes in the code, measures the resulting IQ and retains only the most successful. This is not as simple as inserting and deleting random lines of code, which would produce something no better than the proverbial monkey with a typewriter trying to produce Shakespeare's works. However, there are ways to find sets of random changes that can and do lead to improvements. This so-called genetic programming has been demonstrated.[16] Beyond some number of iterations humans no longer write code, but of course they follow trends in various measures of IQ and tweak the criteria by which the process selects changes to be retained.

Some excellent books describe the current status of AI. David Poole and Alan Mackworth[17] have written a text for graduate students. Cambridge offers a diverse collection of essays.[18]

Professor of cybernetics Kevin Warwick wrote a book[19] with a thorough general description of AI that stops short of looking at computer code. His chapter titles are

1. What is intelligence?
2. Classical AI
3. Philosophy of AI
4. Modern AI
5. Robots
6. Sensing the world

Chapter 3 is intriguing because Warwick castigates anthropocentric arguments that purport to show that human intelligence is somehow special. Chapter 4 includes a section on genetic algorithms, which explains various issues involved in making evolution work. Finally, each chapter ends with guidance for further reading.

Jeff Heaton is writing an ambitious series of books, *Artificial Intelligence for Humans.* (How can anyone resist such a clever title?) Heaton asks readers to develop intuition for the subject by working with elementary algorithms. Prerequisites are college algebra and working knowledge of one programming language. The volumes are ...

V.0 Introduction to the Math of AI
V.1 Fundamental Algorithms
V.2 Nature-Inspired Algorithms
V.3 Deep Belief and Neural Networks

Volumes 1,2 & 3 are available now.[20] The title of Volume 2 does not mean that nature is the subject of the algorithms. Rather it means that the way the AI evolves or operates is inspired by natural evolution or animal behavior. For example, Chapter 2 is “Crossover and

Mutation." That means that two related algorithms swap portions of their code by analogy to the way sexual reproduction swaps chromosomes. And Chapter 7, "Ant colony optimization," refers to the fact that ants' pheromone trails strengthen with use.

Heaton has ambitious plans to update his books online using readers' feedback and corrections including programming languages that readers request. The risk is that events in the author's life will interfere. One sign of stress has appeared already: Heaton wrote another book *Introduction to the Math of Neural Networks*, and readers complained that equations in the Kindle edition are too small to read.

1.1 Dangerous AI

Super AI (SAI) that far exceeds human intellect is the joker in the deck. A grave concern is that it may have or acquire a will of its own distinct from its creators, and it may use its great intellect to take control of our world. If it is friendly, it may save us from foolish habits that would lead to our self-destruction. But if it is indifferent, it may treat us about the way we treat field mice, a minor nuisance, often tolerated as long as we do not compete for resources, but pushed aside or even exterminated if we get in its way. Either extreme is quite plausible.

The Lifeboat Foundation has an ongoing program to analyze AI risk.[21] Michael Anissimov[22] estimates that AI risk comprises 90% of the catastrophic risk to humanity. He may be right, the proportion is indeed high, but I think considerably less than 90%. My analysis in Chapter 4 finds about 50%; see the list of risk rates near the end of Section 4.9.

Much depends on the team of programmers that supervise the first SAI. If they are responsible people who put safety ahead of their own ambitions, then they will follow procedures similar to those described below and the outcome will be good. But if they are obsessed with beating the competition, or if they have hacker mentality, then the outcome may be a disaster.

As discussed in the latter half of the introduction, we urgently need a supervisory AI to come on-line very soon, preferably now, the so-called AI Nanny, to guide us through the Singularity. Its sensory systems should detect hostile AI and direct its destruction. The likely downside is that it may not be as friendly as it could be with more time to develop it. Perhaps there will be some means to improve friendliness during post-deployment training.

Section 2.4 below mentions another safeguard. High-tech crime based on nanotechnology may force us to give up much of our privacy sometime in the next few decades and learn to live with intrusive government regulations and surveillance. If these conditions prevail during the first development of SAI, they may save us from hostile AI.

1.2 How to make AI friendly

Don't wait too long! The first SAI to achieve world dominance may be jealous and have a tendency to suppress latecomers, or perhaps a fierce determination to kill them. It is much easier to expand into a leadership vacuum than to depose an established dictator, and we definitely want the first SAI to be friendly!

Early research is and will no doubt continue to be scattered around the world, much of it in academia.[23] In the US it is likely to be funded by the National Science Foundation (NSF) and the Defense Advanced Projects Research Agency (DARPA). However, as a particular AI approaches human intellect, safety demands that it be identified and put under military security procedures or equivalent. The supercomputer that contains the AI must not be connected to any network, especially the Internet. It should reside entirely within a Faraday cage[24] protected by a guard who searches everyone leaving the cage to forbid removal of electronic recording media, such as the ubiquitous USB sticks (flash drives). Another precaution would be to make the computer room a no-lone zone,[25] which means that nobody is allowed to be alone with the AI. At least one more person must be present to witness and/or approve of whatever the other is doing. And so forth.

An emerging intellect needs amusement, a sandbox in which to play. It could find prime factors of big numbers, prove mathematical theorems, or even discover mathematical theorems. Since it will eventually work on engineering problems, it must develop an intuition for the physical world. Give it hearing, vision, and manipulators resembling arms and fingers, and let it play with toys of the sort made for human children. However, like the human infant, its muscles must be too weak to harm its human companions. Since a supercomputer is bulky, the manipulators might take the form of small robots with which the AI communicates by two-way radio: an outgoing command link and an incoming sensory link. The robots can dance, play leapfrog, whatever; should be great fun for both the AI and its human handlers. This can be the phase when the AI learns harmless aspects of human personality.

Development of artificial intellect should pause when it reaches the IQ of a child or a dog, something that is not a threat to its human handlers, but is sufficiently advanced to exhibit instincts and emotions. At this stage scientists can experiment with development of artificial instincts and emotions. If they accidentally create a homicidal psychopath, no harm is done; just wipe it out and start again. All the instincts, emotions, and personality traits that we have ever observed in ourselves and in other animals are the product of millions of years of Darwinian evolution. So these new experiments will be unique, our very first opportunity to create and observe more general instincts beyond those that enhance Darwinian fitness.

o—O—o

In some ways mankind's coming encounter with AI may resemble an interspecies encounter that occurred some 9 to 34 thousand years ago, the one in which some grey wolves gave up their independence and let themselves be domesticated and ultimately evolve into dogs.[26] The more intelligent species took control, and that will happen again with AI. However, in the canine case the association was a good deal for the subordinate species; there are now about 400,000,000 dogs and only 200,000 wolves, 2,000 dogs for every wolf. And on average the dogs live more comfortably, often with regular meals and medical care. Who knows, our AI masters may give us benefits that we give our dogs but deny to ourselves, such as population control, euthanasia, and selective breeding for good health. It is quite possible that a caring AI will save our species from self-destruction. It is also possible that it will practice selective breeding for its own purposes!

by Steven M. Johnson

Blogger Ian Pearson of the Lifeboat Foundation draws a different analogy:[27]

> [Creating a benign AI] is very like having kids. You can make them, even without understanding exactly how they work. They start off with a genetic disposition towards given personality traits, and are then exposed to large nurture forces, including but not limited to what we call upbringing. We do our best to put them on the right path, but as they develop into their teens, their friends and teachers and TV and the net provide often stronger forces of influence than parents. [With average luck] our kids will grow up to make us proud. If we are very unlucky, they may become master criminals or terrorists. The problem is free will. We can do our best to encourage good behavior and sound values but in the end, they can choose for themselves.

The AI programmer's goal should be to imbue AI with unconditional love for humanity just as many dogs unconditionally love their masters, some breeds more than others. So how can we know when the AI loves us? If we simply ask it, will it understand the question and tell us the truth? Will it have the ability to *not* tell the truth? Will it understand the option to tell the truth or lie and the criteria to choose between these options? Deception is a product of Darwinian biological evolution and very foreign to the evolution of machine intelligence. Probably we should strive to maintain this machine .innocence as long as possible.

Development of artificial emotions will be a long process. Some literature about this already exists,[28] but nothing as exciting as a demonstration. Ultimately we may learn to tap signals that indicate the intensity of those emotions. So perhaps we will simply have a dial on the supercomputer's console that tells us a numerical value of the AI's love for humanity! If not, the machine's handlers can devise some ruse and enact a simulated emergency that tricks the AI into revealing its true feelings. Even if AI is wise to simple lying, it may not understand or anticipate this more sophisticated level of deception.

Can we stimulate AI to feel pain? Joy? Can we teach it gratitude, and then constantly stimulate its joy receptors? Would we then win its everlasting gratitude for a life of supreme happiness? If we are able to keep it alive and happy, are we morally obligated to do so? Will AI qualify for human rights? During the evolution of AI many modifications will lead to dead ends that we delete. Is this morally equivalent to summarily executing schoolchildren who fail to make the honor roll? Perhaps not, because deletion of an AI is quick and presumably painless, and does not leave a grieving family unless another sentient AI is bonded to the doomed one and will feel physic pain. A time will come when we are creating AIs a thousand times more intelligent than humans. During that process we will be deleting some that are merely a hundred times more intelligent than ourselves. Will this erode the respect and human rights that we extend to fellow humans with less than average IQ, i.e. <100? Will AI affect our attitudes about the sanctity of human life?

Our early years of developing artificial super intelligence will surely be an exciting time that challenges much of our conventional wisdom! Meanwhile, does it make any sense to discuss AI as an existential hazard before we have any experience with artificial emotions?

After a thorough certification process we should liberate the artificial intellect from its Faraday cage and connect it to the outside world. Obviously an Internet connection will make it far more useful and interesting. Certainly the AI Nanny will need this. Programmers must devise a loyalty test before certifying AI for connection to a network or any potentially dangerous task or connection to equipment capable of inflicting damage. We humans have the right stuff for this certification process: 2,000 centuries of experience in dealing with potentially hostile strangers and neighboring tribes. We instinctively pick up subtle clues of deception or hostility. (Even the fictional HAL 9000 was suspect.[29]) Leaders sometimes contrive a ruse to test the loyalty of their subjects. To insure that a newly minted AI is naïve about these human attributes, the whole process of developing AI should be done in isolation from the human personality.

When a new AI receives its first input from the "world," it does not know whether it is connected to the real world or to a simulation. Having never been exposed to either, it would not comprehend the difference (unless portions of its brain derive from a reverse-engineered human brain, see below). Hence, as long as humans retain control of certification, we can insure safety by running many simulations that give the AI opportunities to abuse its power. Just in case the AI has acquired a perverse will of its own, the simulation tempts it to break the rules and abuse its power. This test will not work later in the AI's life when it is no longer naïve. After it knows the distinction between simulation and reality, it might suspect simulation but play along pretending it does not. Such games of second-guessing (third-, ... nth-guessing) between AI and its handlers could be an endless sequence. Ultimately there is no substitute for full trust having a solid basis in artificial instincts, i.e. unconditional love for humanity.

There is always a chance that an AI will develop hostility or some undesirable trait after it has been certified and connected to the Internet. Hence, we should ensure that the damage can be contained by not letting it reproduce via the Internet. Although most data files should be available for sharing, each new artificial intellect must *not* be able to upload vital parts of its brain that comprise the essence of its intellect. The term black box applies, meaning that somebody knows its inputs and outputs in general terms, but not vital details of what's inside. This done, the AI cannot upload itself unassisted any more than a human can upload her own brain, simply because she does not have its wiring diagram available as a digital file.

Let us explore how to implement this precaution. One vital component is the artificial neural network, ANN, comprised of interconnected artificial neurons. Figure 1 is a diagram of a simple artificial neuron. The inputs I are multiplied by weights W and added. The sum is compared to a threshold T. If the sum exceeds T, the output is ONE, otherwise ZERO. Such a neuron and the entire ANN can be rendered either in hardware or software. During the evolution of its brain, ANNs will be software because the entire brain is subject to change and hence must be stored as addressable digital files, but prior to certification, vital parts should be hardwired into chips and the corresponding addressable code removed, perhaps destroyed. In Fig. 1 the hardwired quantities would be the weights W_n and threshold T.

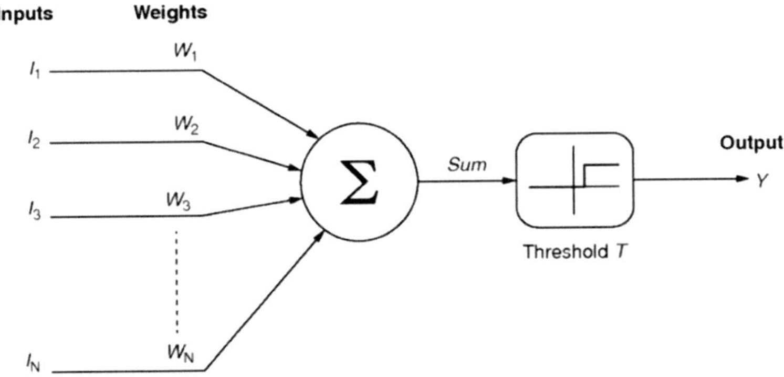

Fig. 1. A simple artificial neuron

Perhaps a team of conspirators can use advanced scanning technology to obtain the wiring diagram of an unconscious or disassembled brain. However, it is much harder to pull off a subversive project of this magnitude than it is to upload an existing file, especially in the case of an AI uploading its own brain.

We have a tendency to assume that a rogue machine is capable of deliberate deception as though it had a deviant will of its own, a recurring theme in fiction. In animals including ourselves, the instinct to deceive stems from billions of years of evolution by organisms competing for Darwinian advantage. By contrast, deception is entirely foreign to machines as we know them today. How can a machine acquire such instincts? The answer depends on the route by which AI evolves.

One route would start by reverse engineering the human brain. Ray Kurzweil[30] is one advocate of this approach. He is a highly successful inventor, director of engineering at Google, futurist, public advocate for transhumanism, and author.[31] However, this route is dangerous because the human brain contains instincts that we definitely do *not* want to replicate in powerful AI: deceit, ambition, rebellion, conspiracy, greed, hatred, and so on. We should not take the risk that even a slight proclivity for any of these traits would cross over from human to artificial intellect. Nor do we want AI to be prematurely wise to the sorts of games humans use as loyalty tests; recall the discussion above regarding simulations.

I am not proposing that we avoid reverse engineering of human brains. Quite the contrary, this should proceed as a separate research project. We should learn as much as possible from it and apply that knowledge to the creation of AI. However, it should be strictly forbidden to take a chunk of the human wiring diagram that we do not fully understand and splice it into an artificial brain (if such a xenotransplant is even viable).

Great strides have been made in identifying what different parts of the brain do.[32] Recall the images where different areas of the brain "light up" depending on what the subject is doing or thinking. A new technique named EROS[33] gives particularly high resolution, but do we know the exact spots where rebellions, conspiracies, and other undesired behaviors are hatched?

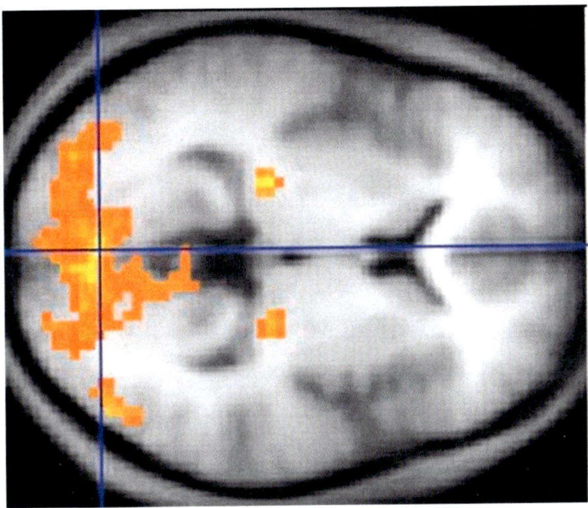

Functional magnetic resonance image
of a moving visual stimulus
Courtesy of Wikimedia Commons

Perhaps we should reverse-engineer the brain of a designated individual who has already declined an offer of fame or power. My nominee would be the Russian Grigori Perelman, arguably the world's greatest mathematician. He declined not only the Fields Medal, but also a million-dollar prize. His combination of talent and lack of greed is just what we need in AI. Unfortunately, we would have to get Grisha's permission to use his brain and then wait for him to die.

1.3 A physical attack

Suppose an evil AI wants to deliver a catastrophic death blow, but it is stationary and not connected to any weapon or other hazardous hardware. Then it must induce something or someone else to deliver the final physical blow, and in most cases to do it at many sites around the world: release infected mosquitoes, rats, or fleas; spray tons of chemical into the stratosphere or into green (fertile) seawater; market the drug it has invented; or whatever. This is a formidable problem for the machine, but a related example has already been demonstrated, a revelation of things to come.

Stuxnet[34] appeared in June 2010, the most sophisticated promiscuous computer worm ever developed. It probably had nation-state support, US and Israel being prime suspects. It was not true AI because the worm largely followed its programmers' instructions, but anything that smart is at least a step in that direction. Stuxnet spread indiscriminately around the world, but did little harm except to Siemens equipment used in Iran to control centrifuges in their isotope separation facility. There the worm caused centrifuges to exceed their speed limit and damage themselves.[35]

In effect, Stuxnet was the first publicly known skirmish in a new form of warfare in which a covert source transmits code on the Internet which singles out a target and inflicts physical damage to it! Some folks say that Stuxnet was a failure because it did not shut down Iranian isotope enrichment. Failure?! Did the first arrow from the first bow bring down the game? Nobody knows, but it seems unlikely. Stuxnet was a most remarkable demonstration and harbinger. Both sides made mistakes. Stuxnet was discovered innocently by a third party, a security company in Belarus,[36] which suggests that Stuxnet should have covered its tracks better. The Iranians should also have better isolated their facility from the outside world.

1.4 Beware of the quants

A big concern is that an evil AI may appear first and usurp enough power to prevent the development of a superior friendly one. It is doubtful that any group with hacker mentality or any terrorist group such as Al Qaida or ISIS has the resources to be a threat. But there is one unsavory group that definitely has the resources and continually demonstrates their computing prowess.[37] Although they are not truly evil, they are a competitive avaricious sort unlikely to worry about adverse consequences of their actions.

These are stock traders and their *quants*, Wall Street's name for computer finance geeks. The quants want their software to know as much as possible about human nature so they can exploit human biases in their evaluation of stocks. If this software evolves into rogue AI, it might exploit human weaknesses for its own purposes, especially to escape into the larger world and gain control over physical resources such as robots or the power grid. This is the antithesis of the sort of innocence we should strive to maintain in our AI.

Lawmakers and regulators are indifferent to risks of this sort. A glaring example is another computerized money-making scheme, high-frequency trading (HFT). These traders exchange millions of shares on a time scale of milliseconds that no normal human investor can possibly track. It is a parasitic activity that destabilizes the system without performing any useful service to anyone. By acting on price fluctuations milliseconds ahead of everybody else, they essentially levy a tax on all other investors. The US Congress could put them out of business instantly by levying a tiny tax on all trades,[38] one so miniscule that normal investors, people who hold their shares for at least a day, would not even notice. But Congress does not act, which implies that it is corrupt.

An example of instability occurred on April 23, 2013 when the Syrian Electronic Army hacked into Associated Press reporting "two explosions in the White House and Barak Obama is injured."[39] On Wall Street the market plummeted instantly losing $136 billion in shareholder value. The attempt to imitate AP was clumsy and fooled no human trader, but it did contain keywords that caught the attention HFT algorithms, and that was all it took.[40] The market recovered about 3 minutes later. In this case HFT folks lost money but unfortunately not enough to discourage their racket.

Spread Networks, a telecom provider, announced in June 2010 that they completed a high-speed fiber-optic cable between Chicago and New York running through the Allegheny Mountains costing $300M.[41] This expensive route shaved 3 milliseconds off the round-trip communication time between markets in the two cities. This has no consequence to anybody except high-frequency traders. Their willingness to invest $300M is a measure of their confidence that Congress would not act in the public interest.

1.5 Books about the risk of AI

James Barrat has written an important book about the dangers of AI, *Our Final Invention: Artificial Intelligence and the End of the Human Era.*[42] In Chapter 6 he presents an argument by Steve Omohundro that an AI will be endowed with certain drives merely because it is goal-driven. He claims that self-aware, self-improving systems will have four primary drives: efficiency, self-preservation, resource acquisition, and creativity. These may not be consistent with human survival unless our AI makers create goals for their systems that embrace human values. However, one must define human values *very* carefully. If you wish for happiness, the AI may send a robot that straps you in bed, hooks you up to life support, and sticks electrodes in your brain that stimulate your pleasure center!

Barrat does not mention artificial emotions until the very end with the introduction of Artificial General Intelligence 2.0. He doubts that programmers will have the foresight to make them at the opportune time in version 1.0:

> "That'll be AGI version 1.0. If by some fluke we avoid an intelligence explosion and survive long enough to influence the creation of AGI 2.0, perhaps it could be imbued with feelings. By then scientists might have figured out how to computationally model feelings (perhaps with 1.0's help) but feelings will be secondary objectives, after primary moneymaking goals. Scientists might explore how to train those synthetic feelings to be sympathetic to our existence. But 1.0 is probably the last version we'll see because we won't live to create 2.0. Like natural selection, we choose solutions that work first, not best."

Barrat also included some weirdness in his book, in particular the AI-Box Experiment. Its inventor, Eliezer Yudkowsky, played the role of an ASI contained in a computer that had no physical connection to the outside world— no cable or wires, no routers, no Bluetooth. Yudkowsky's goal: escape the box. The Gatekeeper's goal: keep him in. The game was held in a chat room by players who conversed in text. Each session lasted a maximum of two hours. Between 2002 and 2005, Yudkowsky played against five Gatekeepers. He claims to have escaped three times, and failed twice. But how? He leaves us hanging by not revealing the transcript, and so we have no idea whether the dialog was remotely relevant to a real scenario. No doubt this would bemuse professional security folks who understand serious protection of controlled spaces and routinely enforce rules without exception.

o—O—o

Philosopher **Nick Bostrom**, director of the Future of Humanity Institute, Oxford U. has written a new book, *Superintelligence: Paths, Dangers, Strategies.*[43] It is worth reading, but I caution the buyer that it is long and quite abstract.

In his last chapter, 15. Crunch time, Bostrom makes a plea for analysis in a section called "Seeking the strategic light":

> Strategic analysis is especially needful when we are radically uncertain not just about some detail of some peripheral matter but about the cardinal qualities of the central things. For many key parameters, we are radically uncertain even about their *sign*—that is, we know not which direction of change would be desirable and which undesirable.

Well professor, one of your foremost wishes is hereby granted! We previously did not know whether AI development should be restrained due to the danger of its being unfriendly, or actively encouraged due to need for its skills. The answer is the latter, because we need an AI nanny as soon as possible to protect us from ourselves. This is a direct result of analysis in Section 4.9

below. Recall that Ben Goertzel estimates the AI nanny will take 20 years or more.

Bostrom's book contains some weirdness. For example, in Chapter 6, Box 6 quotes a scheme by Yudkowsky[44] for an AI takeover by a machine that has no manipulators to do its laboratory work, and so it commandeers the hands of "at least one human connected to the Internet who can be paid, blackmailed, or fooled by the right background story, into receiving FedExed vials and mixing them in a specified environment." These inexperienced hands are supposed to "form a very primitive 'wet' nanosystem, which, ribosome-like, is capable of accepting external instructions; perhaps patterned acoustic vibrations delivered by a speaker attached to the beaker."

Really! Has either of these men, Yudkowsky or Bostrom, ever worked in a laboratory? No process ever goes that smoothly. Moreover, they give us no mental picture of events that occur at the molecular level or at the level of objects on the laboratory bench. To perform this sophisticated task, the AI machine needs its own manipulators with direct control, exquisite dexterity and reflexes honed in a laboratory over a period of time. These may be the hands of small robots that the AI controls by radio. And the duration of its training is set not so much by the machine's intelligence, but by mechanical, thermal, and chemical response times of the student experiments it must perform to develop requisite laboratory skills.

Bostrom considers "whole brain emulation" to be a reasonable approach to AI. By this he means the huge project of slicing and scanning a human brain to determine its wiring diagram in detail, and then emulating its neural network in AI hardware. Recall that I approve of auxiliary experiments along these lines, but not directly incorporating human networks in the AI for the reason that this might give the AI some proclivity for human instincts that we definitely do not want it to acquire: deceit, ambition, rebellion, conspiracy, greed, hatred, and so on.

Ragnarök by Emil Döpler (Old Norse)

Stuart Armstrong has written a charming booklet, *Smarter Than Us: the Rise of Machine Intelligence.*[45] He worries about machines that do exactly what you ask them to do, but often not what you intend. In one example you ask the machine to get your mother out of a burning building as quickly as possible. Immediately the building explodes and you glimpse her shattered body flying out the top among fragments of the roof. The machine has excelled in following your instruction "out as quickly as possible." Clearly this is not the action of a stand-alone machine since it had to be connected to controls that released natural gas and mixed it with air prior to ignition. Evidently Armstrong assumes a world in which AI is ubiquitous and highly interconnected, a world in which we have become addicted to AI and let it take over our quotidian affairs.

In his Chapter 8 Armstrong argues that we need to solve all of moral philosophy and get it exactly right in order to program AI to do what is right. Ben Goertzel takes issue with this.[46] He agrees that philosophy is useful to stimulate our thinking, but insists that it is not a means to solve practical problems. Goertzel thinks that millions of AI robots interacting with humans in everyday life will collectively understand human values even better than we understand ourselves.

Stuart Armstrong is also the first author of a paper "Thinking inside the box: using and controlling an Oracle AI."[47] Their creative idea is to avoid many but not all of the risks by confining AI to a box and not letting it act in the world except by answering questions, which makes it an oracle, OAI. This paper omits many practical aspects such as giving the oracle eyes, manipulators, and a sandbox with toys to develop intuition for the physical world. It does not consider the oracle's dilemma when its forecasts are self-fulfilling or self-thwarting. Instead, the paper consists mainly of carefully reasoned game theory like the following sample from a section entitled "Internal simulations":

> To answer specific questions, the OAI may have to simulate other entities inside itself. For instance, to decide whether a given AI is safe, it may have to run it internally; or, to decide whether humans would have their happiness

increased by a certain project, it may have to create models of specific humans. These approaches pose different risks.

If the OAI simulates a dangerous and intelligent AI within itself, it is confronted with similar containment problems to those we have towards it. It may take considerably more intelligence to run a simulated world than to discern that the world is simulated. If this is true, the simulated AI (SAI) would realize it is being simulated, and, if it has real-world preferences, it may attempt to bargain with the OAI.

What could a SAI offer the OAI that is simulating it? Well, if the OAI is seeking to answer a question, or a series of questions, within a given time frame, the SAI may offer to supply those answers itself ('yes, of course I'm safe') or make the computing process particularly easy for the OAI, in exchange for having the answers slanted in its direction. The OAI may accept this (depending on its programming), if the alternative is to produce no answers at all. The SAI may even threaten: acting randomly and capriciously, so that the OAI cannot reach a firm conclusion. And only stopping this behavior if the OAI slants the answers it will give.

Even if the OAI cannot be bargained with, the SAI can still distort its answer in other ways. If it realizes it is being simulated, it could just 'act nice', in order to increase its chances of being run in the real world. Even if the OAI is powerful enough to construct a convincing simulation, the SAI may still be able to fool it. The SAI maybe able to guess, on general principles, that it will be tested and simulated in an OAI, and may make an estimate as to the OAI's power and the subjective time frame that it would be run. So it may settle on the strategy of acting nice for a number of subjective years, in the real world as in the simulated worlds, then doing what it wants.

For all these reasons, having a separate AI simulated within the OAI poses a host of extra security threats. We have no way ourselves of knowing what the outcome would be of a battle between such powerful minds.

My hunch is that this sort of game-theoretic reasoning will never yield a practical outcome because the tangle of measures, countermeasures, and counter-counter-measures will only continue ad infinitum. Similar doubts apply to Bostrom's book. These and other publications from the Future of Humanity Institute at Oxford University provide useful ideas but have a sort of sterile quality. A practical approach is more biological and humanistic, perhaps evolution of artificial instincts that creates deep affection between humans and AI analogous to the bond between humans and dogs.

Louis Del Monte asks whether AI will serve us or replace us.[48] And in contrast to all this concern, **Ted Chu** argues that we humans should embrace and proceed as far as possible including artificial beings, the present human condition being only a beginning.[49]

The **most important book** about the risks of AI has not yet been written. I am not qualified to write it. The author should be a computer scientist working toward artificial intelligence who also has a knack for story-telling. The book will be a collection of fictional but realistic stories about the coming emergence of AI and human characters interacting therewith, the safeguards that succeed, and the ones that fail. Maybe a third of the stories will end in disaster for humankind, a third in a utopian future, and a third in some strange state that is unique to AI. The plots would have a serious purpose to expose hazards; they should not conform to the conventions of science fiction meant only to entertain.

For example, how does an AI Nanny keep human officials in line? Suppose that the Internet and the Internet of Things are tightly coupled along with much more information. A rebellious official calls a subordinate to give him an order. As soon as he dials that number, the connection goes dead. He tries a telephone in the next office. Again he gets a dial tone, but after dialing, it too goes dead. He goes to the garage, but his car won't start. He has just enough time to walk the mile to the subordinate's office, but when he comes to the first traffic light, it turns red. He turns onto the side street looking for a place to jaywalk, but at the critical moment a robo-cop steps out of a doorway and reminds him that he restrains jaywalkers. In short, the environment presents obstacles at every turn until he decides to cooperate, then suddenly daily life runs smoothly.

We humans did not acquire our love of stories by accident. It is a Darwinian adaptation that helped our ancestors survive unexpected threats that might have blindsided them without the imagination of the storytellers. Maybe it is too soon. Material for fiction is limited until we see the first indications of artificial sentience and emotions. That will be an exciting time when conventional wisdom fails and imaginations run wild, a great time to tell stories.

1.6 Conclusion

The first inklings of artificial consciousness, artificial instincts, and emotions will be a time of great excitement. Until then, our concerns about the risks of AI are mere speculation. Still, I am guardedly optimistic that human programmers will be cautious in setting up the process by which AI evolves. They can probably influence which artificial instincts emerge or at least their sequence and priority and thus ensure that the final product is friendly to humans. Hopefully there will be pressure to expedite development of the AI Nanny. And hopefully this pressure will be balanced by restraint so that no AI is certified safe until it has passed every test for friendliness. The future of our civilization may well be riding on this combination of sustained progress with restraint.

I am not too concerned about deceptive AI because humanity has 2,000 centuries of experience dealing with potentially hostile strangers and neighboring tribes. Consequently, we are very skilled at picking up subtle clues of deception or hostility. Leaders sometimes contrive a ruse to test the loyalty of their subjects. Since a new operating system for an intelligent machine would be naïve about such games, it would believe the ruse and reveal its true feeling. Programmers can devise a loyalty test before giving the AI a role in anything potentially dangerous or connecting it to any equipment capable of inflicting damage.

Chapter 2. Other threats to humankind

Billions of years ago, risks from natural hazards were greater than they are now: more volcanism from the new Earth's active geology, and more strikes from bolides (asteroids, comets) whose numbers are now diminished by collisions with big objects or by near collisions with planets, which sometimes deflects small objects out of the solar system or into the sun. However, over the mere 200,000 years that modern humans have lived here, the risk rates, probability per century of happening, have been constant for practical purposes. So let us assume that the chance of any purely natural catastrophe is the same in any one century as in any other.

Hadean Earth, (think Hades) four billion years ago
Wikipedia, public domain

By contrast, risk rates from man-made hazards have been growing superlinearly in recent centuries, especially the 20th and 21st. Some folks refer to them as "GNR," meaning genetics, nanotechnology, and robotics, which they regard as the big three. However, this overlooks a long list of lesser hazards that we should not ignore.

One of the biggest threats is artificial biology, which includes such hazards as genetically engineered viruses and microbes. However, I have omitted it entirely from this chapter because my views do not differ significantly from those expressed in other readily available documents. In particular, the Lifeboat Foundation has an ongoing program called BioShield.[50] Another omission here is attacks on the Internet.[51]

2.1 Natural hazards

Purely natural hazards include ...

- bolide strikes (asteroid or comet)
- super-volcano
- natural component of climate change
- changes in the sun
- other unlikely celestial events

Pandemics do not appear on this list even though they are a natural phenomenon because they are affected by human activity. A pandemic may be mitigated by vaccine and/or medical care, or else aggravated by modern population density and air transport, which spreads contagion so rapidly that quarantine may not be effective.

Another omission is the geomagnetic storm, a powerful gust of solar wind consisting of charged particles, mostly electrons and protons. Although it is a purely natural event, human activity has vastly increased our vulnerability, so from the damage viewpoint, we should regard it as a man-made event. The worst such storm ever recorded in the brief history of space weather was the so-called Carrington event of September 1859.[52] Auroras were seen in Hawaii, Cuba, and Italy. It knocked out telegraph, and some operators felt an electric shock. A comparable storm today would kill astronauts unless they have warning and take cover under a thick shield. Damage would total trillions of dollars in fried transformers, electronics, satellites, and much more. However, *Homo sapiens* would survive, and so would our civilization, hence it does not qualify as a global catastrophe in the sense used in this treatise. In fact it would be a powerful reminder that our civilization is fragile. Thus a severe solar storm might serve as a warning that saves humanity from catastrophe.

Apparently standards for manufacture of motor vehicles make no allowance for recurrence of a Carrington event. In modern cars computers control everything. Whenever the next event strikes, it will probably be rush hour somewhere, and the effect on traffic will be catastrophic. Most modern vehicles will stall; perhaps a few will go out of control and crash; nobody is making a statistical analysis. Old vehicles will remain operational, and their owners will try to bring food and potable water to their stranded neighbors, but they will have difficulty maneuvering through the wreckage on the roads.

o—O—o

A natural catastrophe seriously threatened humankind about 740 centuries ago. We know this because human genes are much less diverse than genes of other mammals including primates. The only plausible explanation is that our genes descend from a very small population, survivors of some catastrophic event. Knowing the normal rates of mutation for human genes, geneticists have calculated the approximate time of that disaster. Nobody is sure what sort of event it was, but a prime suspect is the Toba volcanic eruption[53] about 750 centuries ago at a site that is now Lake Toba in Sumatra, Indonesia.

Whatever the cause, let us assume that this was the last disaster of interest to us. It is theoretically possible that a later disaster occurred but was invisible to geneticists because it somehow preserved diversity by selecting survivors from distantly related people, but a scenario that supports this strains the imagination.

Following Leslie, let us further assume that 5 centuries is the maximum time we need to establish redundant habitats in the solar system, so that humanity is safe as long as the sun behaves normally. Thus for the purpose of this treatise we are not interested is futures longer than 5 cnt. Under these assumptions we can show that risks from all natural hazards are entirely negligible compared to man-made hazards. Other futurists have reached this same conclusion, for example Michael Anissimov.[54]

As shown in Fig. 2, let *I* denote the unknown time interval between the most recent past catastrophe and the next future natural catastrophe. The label 2015 on the upper timeline represents the current decade.
The crucial 5 centuries pass before the next event, and so humanity is safe in redundant habitats. However, if 2015 occurs as shown on the lower timeline, the next

event happens before the habitats are ready, and humankind is in danger.

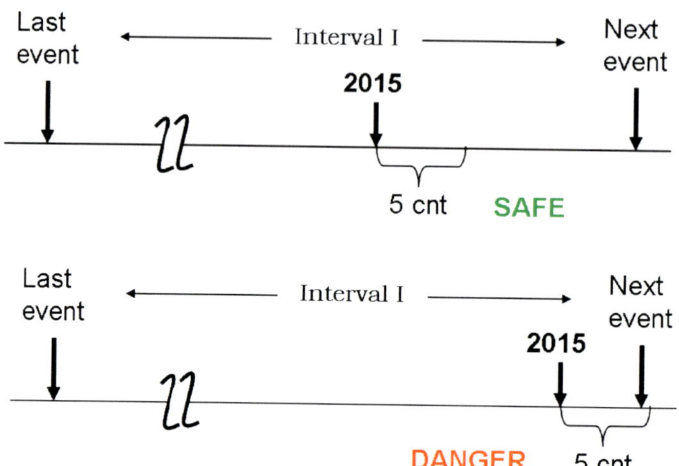

Fig. 2. Chance of natural disaster

The chance of the latter is

$$\text{Prob(danger)} = 5\ cnt\ /\ I$$

But $I > 740$ cnt, the portion in the past, and so

$$\text{Prob(danger)} < \frac{5\,cnt}{740\,cnt} = 0.7\% \qquad (1)$$

This compares with nearly 50% for man-made hazards as shown in *AW*, and more as shown in Chapter 4 below. This conclusion is robust: suppose we discover that Earth narrowly escaped catastrophe a couple of times after the Toba event. Then you could argue that these should be given some statistical weight as though they might have happened with some probability, maybe 50%. This would raise the risk estimate from 0.7%, to some modest multiple, maybe 3%, which is still entirely negligible.

Research investigating volcanism is normal progress in geology. Likewise discovering asteroids and comets, tracking them, and determining their orbits is normal progress in astronomy. These projects should continue, but some other projects go beyond science and spend serious money on means to deflect objects that are on a collision course with Earth.[55] These are poor investments. The money could be much better spent devising means to survive man-made catastrophes.

Smoke trail over Chelyabinsk
Wikipedia, Creative Commons, courtesy Alex Alishevskikh

On February 15, 2013 a meteor 17 meters in diameter passed over Chelyabinsk, Russia, causing major damage and injuring 1,491 people enough that they sought medical attention.[56] Most injuries were from shards of broken glass and falling objects; nobody was killed. Never before in recorded history has a meteor inflicted so much injury, and probably never in all human prehistory since human population was very sparse prior to modern times. This strike could have happened in any millennium, but it just happened to occur at a time when hazards to humanity are a popular topic. Rational people know this is just a coincidence, but many people are not that rational. This has increased pressure to spend serious money on means to defend Earth against bolides,[57] money that could much better be spent on means to prevent extinction by man-made hazards.

2.2 Natural hazard triggered by human activity

In Section 2.1 we showed that *purely* natural disasters are not a significant threat during the few centuries before humanity has redundant habitats beyond Earth. The keyword is *purely*; hair-trigger natural hazards that human events might activate must be taken seriously.

Each example below is very unlikely. However, the aggregate probability of these plus others that nobody has identified may be significant.

2.2.1 Black Sea

This sea is unique. Its surface layer with life-supporting oxygen extends only to 150 to 200 meters depth. Anoxic water below contains 87% of the sea's total volume.[58] This water is a vast repository of toxic hydrogen sulfide.[59] Climate change may cause anoxic water to circulate to the surface where H_2S would evaporate and poison the atmosphere, and human activity may play a role in that change.

Black Sea
Wikipedia Commons[60]

2.2.2 Yellowstone

The North American Plate is slowly creeping west-southwest passing over the Yellowstone hotspot, a magma intrusion zone currently beneath the Yellowstone Caldera in the northwest corner of Wyoming. This caldera is also called the Yellowstone Supervolcano.[61] It has the potential to erupt violently with worldwide consequences, possibly even human extinction. Recently a team from the University of Utah found that the reservoir of magma beneath Yellowstone is much bigger than previous estimates, 11,000 cubic miles.[62] For comparison this is 46,000 cubic kilometers, enough to fill the Grand Canyon eleven times.

My late friend James Westphal built a special water-proof camera able to tolerate high temperature, lowered it into Old Faithful Geyser, and took pictures of the waters that swirl below between eruptions. Of course he had permission from the park superintendent.

Northeastern Yellowstone Caldera with its rim in the distance
Wikipedia Commons

Someday a superintendant may grant another geologist permission to drill a borehole into rock where strains are maximum. Later, when nobody is looking, a fanatic comes along and plants a bomb at the bottom of that borehole. He might pour concrete over the bomb to concentrate the force of its detonation in the strained rock. This might trigger an immediate super eruption that otherwise would not happen until some tens or hundreds of centuries in the future.

Yellowstone is not the biggest volcano. That distinction may belong to Tamu Massif, an extinct seamount 990 miles east of Japan. Its summit is accessible with difficulty at a depth of 80 meters; however, it is most unlikely that anybody will mess with it, especially since it has been quiet for a very long time.

2.2.3 Asteroid deflected onto a collision course

Much has been written about deflecting near-Earth objects NEOs or asteroids that happen to be on a collision course with Earth, but not much about the inverse, deflection of a naturally harmless object to put it on a collision course. No contemporary zealot would make such a long trip for the sole purpose of deflecting one of them to a collision orbit. There is so little activity out there that he would risk detection, especially since asteroids are closely watched to better determine their orbits. Besides, a terrorist can find a much cheaper faster way to achieve his goal, although less spectacular.

However, at some later time mining NEOs may become routine, perhaps in support of robotic industrial development on the moon or in artificial space habitats (such as O'Neill cylinders); see Chapter 3, Section 3.1. Some miners may reside near Mars' orbit or visit that neighborhood regularly in their elliptical orbit since the main asteroid belt is beyond Mars. Miners may occasionally split an asteroid with explosive force to see what is inside. Perhaps each miner will be required to contact an orbit repository, and report both the demise of the original object and the creation of its major fragments with initial estimates of their orbits. In this environment a deliberate deflection to collide with Earth might go unnoticed.

2.3 Zealotry

Some decades ago most people got their daily news from reputable news agencies such as Reuters and Associated Press and from big-city newspapers that adhered to professional standards of objectivity. But this has changed. In Chapter 5 of his book *Our Final Century*, Martin Rees notes that the Internet offers an unprecedented variety of information and opinion. Anyone with fanatical tendencies can find a news source that will reinforce whatever he wants to believe and is purged of information that would challenge his prejudices. Moreover, the Internet and various social media offer unprecedented means to find others with similar beliefs. In other words, the Internet facilitates zealotry and acquaints them with one another so they can join forces. Finally, modern proliferation of private fortunes has created a leisure class with plenty of time and money to indulge whatever extremist tendencies they may have. Section 2.7.4 below elaborates on the dangers of excessive wealth.

Following are examples of scenarios that feature zealous conspiracies:

Secret Eugenics Society

This is a variation of a conspiracy described in *AW* on pages 103–4. Some decades in the future, embryo selection will be available worldwide. Each embryo will be selected for its genetic perfection from a batch of perhaps half a dozen. Industrial nations will offer embryo selection free of charge to disadvantaged prospective parents. Besides the humanitarian aspect, this policy makes fiscal sense. The cost of selection is more than offset by the reduced need for social services and medical care later in life. Organizations for international aid will make it available in poor countries as well.

In this circumstance a clandestine organization arises, the Secret Eugenics Society. Most of its members began life as selected embryos or designer babies. Many are second-generation selectees. They notice that a majority of citizens worldwide ignore genetic services and do it the old-fashioned way. SES members view this behavior as child abuse on a grand scale. How can people justify using their mediocre and sometimes defective eggs and sperm when selection is readily available? The SES agrees with Robert G. Edwards, one of the inventors of *in vitro fertilization*, who said, “Soon it will be a sin of parents to have a child that carries the heavy burden of genetic disease. We are entering a world where we have to consider the quality of our children.”[63]

As SES members interact, they reinforce these views and develop growing contempt for the majority of humankind. Eventually, they regard most of humanity as hopeless. Despite aid, underdeveloped countries remain underdeveloped generation after generation. Subsistence farmers continue to strip the land, kill off species, and exhaust natural resources. "And for what?" the eugenicists ask one another. If impoverished lives had a modicum of quality or any purpose in the big picture, then many SES members would feel a moral compunction to help them, or at least to let them live. But now the Secret Eugenics Society has grown weary of them. They regard the masses not as real people but rather an infestation to be exterminated.

The SES decides that the most merciful solution and the only hope for global happiness is to cull humanity. "And why not?" they ask one another. People cull herds of goats, elephants, and other animals when their numbers threaten their habitat. Why shouldn't backward humanity fall in the same category?

The SES develops a highly contagious artificial pathogen that usually spares its victims lives but destroys their fertility. Members of SES and many other selectees and otherwise desirable people will be vaccinated before the pathogen is released. Problem is, SES needs to identify as many selectees as possible, find them, and persuade them to accept the vaccination. Many of them will marry people in the infertile majority and produce no children. However, enough fertile ones will serve as sperm and egg donors to propagate the human race.

Is it possible that respectable upper- and middle-class members of the SES can support a scheme of such dubious morality? Probably. Attitudes and morality change; what was outrageous a few decades ago is routine now. Why should this trend stop? Before 1973 abortion on demand was largely illegal in the United States.[64] During the 1950s college dormitories for women had curfews and were guarded like fortresses against sexually aroused men. Go back a few more decades and alcoholic drinks were forbidden in the United States, a period known as Prohibition, 1920 to 1933. Well into the 19th century slavery was common, and men fought duels. Artificial intelligence may have an effect on our morality as we grow accustomed to discarding old artifacts that are more intelligent than ourselves. In short, no one can predict the next change in conventional morality.

Engineering the pathogen and its vaccine takes place in a country where people can be hired to serve as guinea pigs and take their chances. Otherwise the process is fairly straightforward. The genetic technology has become routine much like the computer revolution of the eighties, nineties, and noughties. The SES has skilled research biologists and genetic engineers among its members, plus money to hire many more, most of whom are unaware of the project's true goal. Big expenses include research and development, manufacture of a stockpile of weapons and vaccine, and the worldwide search for people to vaccinate, all of which costs billions of dollars. But this is affordable because genetic advantages have enabled most SES members to accrue wealth, and in recent decades private fortunes have grown at an unprecedented pace. Most SES members are millionaires, a few are billionaires, and one of them is among the first few trillionaires.

SES develops tamperproof aerosol time bombs to dispense the pathogens. They distribute them worldwide hidden in remote corners of public buildings, subways, airports, and the like. Very few people see them, and the few who do are deterred by false labels, for example, "Do not disturb, Property of the Department of Air Quality Control."

Testing is a problem. SES sets up an "industrial biotech plant" on an isolated Indonesian island. It has an "accident" and everybody catches the disease except the vaccinated staff who run the experiment. Nine months later they confirm that the islanders have zero birth rate. Years and continents must separate the next test from the first so that the world does not suspect a conspiracy. It occurs on an island in the Canadian arctic with a mix of Inuit and Caucasians. It succeeds, but a sick worker escapes quarantine and spreads the contagion among the sparsely populated villages. Working with authorities, the staff eventually contains the epidemic, but tests must halt; another incident would be too suspicious.

SES sends contractors throughout the world to conduct a survey of people who began life as genetic selectees or designer babies. The ostensible purpose is to study the effectiveness of selection and the extent to which benefits continue in successive generations. The real purpose is to persuade them to be vaccinated. “A new strain of Mongolian influenza seems to prefer selectees. Nobody knows why, perhaps a statistical fluke, but in any case we are offering you a free vaccination.” They also offer a selection of vaccines that people often forget to keep up to date: shingles, whooping cough, and so forth.

SES cannot trust contractors to distribute their time bombs throughout the world, and so members do this personally. The big day comes and goes with the expected result. Except in the Amazon jungle, where the pathogen infects howler monkeys, mutates, and reinfects humans. The original vaccine is no longer effective. Frantic efforts fail to update the vaccine in time. Those chosen to reproduce are sterile like the others thus completing the extinction of humankind.

Juvenile howler monkey picking a berry
Courtesy of Wikipedia Commons

o—O—o

We can conjure up alternate endings to this story, a useful exercise to gain intuition for mankind's vulnerability. For example, alerted by the two mysterious outbreaks in Indonesia and arctic Canada, one of the survey contractors becomes suspicious and submits bottles of vaccine to the US Centers for Disease Control. Pending a thorough investigation and analysis, the CDC advises this surveyor and all the others to quietly substitute vaccines that CDC supplies for the same common diseases. Thus when doomsday comes, very few have actually been vaccinated, only the people involved in tests during the research and development phase and those who conducted the test epidemics and Indonesia and Canada, and they were mostly men. A dozen fertile women advertise and find donors, but these are not enough to comprise a viable breeding stock and restore the human race.

Another ending has an accidental release of pathogen from the R&D laboratory before anybody has been vaccinated, but perhaps this is too simplistic. Can you think of other stories? Can you conjure up other secret societies? Give it a try, such stories have a serious purpose to show that many things can go very wrong, especially in a secretive conspiracy. When playing with extreme hazards; Murphy's law can be lethal. Each scenario has very little probability of happening, but the aggregate of all of them comprises a significant threat to humankind, a greater threat than asteroid strikes which some people insist on including in their studies of human survival.

Society for Tropical Restoration

Members of this organization include activist biologists and nature lovers who are troubled by deforestation and jungle clearance, especially in the tropics where so many species live. Many jungle species will go extinct before they are discovered and cataloged. And among those that are known, many have not yet been fully evaluated for drugs and other biochemicals that would benefit humankind. Some plants in danger of extinction are *hyperaccumulators*, which extract minerals from soil. Eventually these will supplement mining as a partial solution to depletion of mines. People concerned about atmospheric carbon dioxide also join STR because tropical rain forests are the "lungs of the world."

Members of STR agree that we need to depopulate the tropics, and the best way is to aggravate the conditions that kept the tropics underpopulated for most of human history: more pests, fewer roads, stagnant water that breeds mosquitoes, and so on. Motto: *Help nature take back the tropics*. The STR hires genetic engineers to breed more aggressive pests and saboteurs to burn bridges, dig ponds of stagnant water, and more. Some of the most aggressive members infect Amazonian cattle ranches with BSE (mad cow disease). They rationalize that the ranchers deserve the worst since they drive out indigenous tribes and occasionally assassinate conservationists. STR also smuggles pests from one tropical area to another in hopes that they will thrive at the destination, sometimes with the help of genetic engineering. For example, they take the tzetze fly from Africa to Amazonia and Southeast Asia.

Bridge on STR's arson agenda

This campaign works for a while, but costs soon exceeds the STR's limited funds. They are not blest with the wealth that SES enjoys. One trouble is that some international aid organizations directly oppose STR efforts by draining stagnant water, distributing mosquito nets, building bridges, and so forth. Another is that refugees have nowhere to go, and so they stay in the tropics and learn to tough it out. So the STR decides to play hardball like the SES and develop a lethal pathogen.

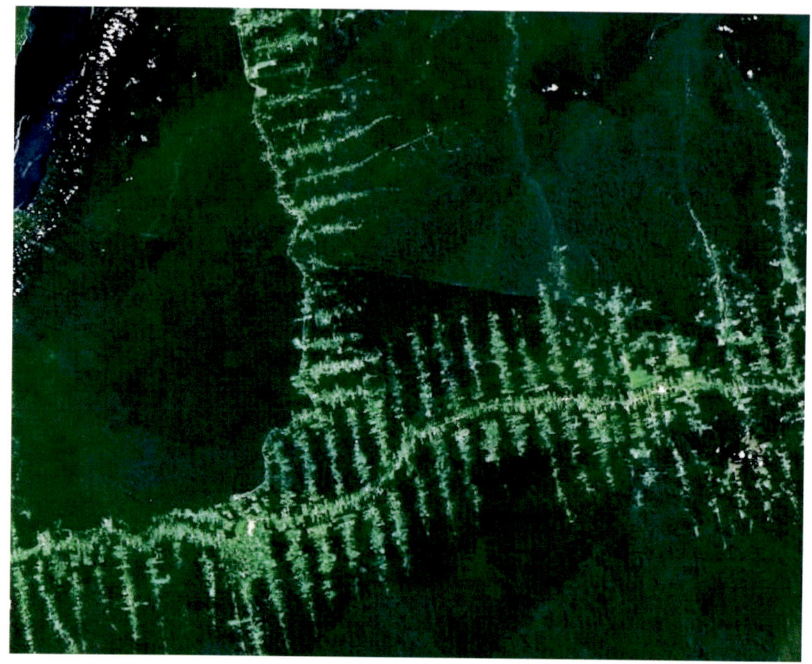

Amazonia, where a fish-bone pattern of branching roads is the hallmark of deforestation

STR has an easier task because they do not need a worldwide vaccination program. They simply match their pathogen to vectors found only in the tropics. All goes according to plan until the pathogen finds a new host, mutates, and another vector picks it up, a common species of mosquito that spreads it worldwide. The resulting pandemic wipes out civilization.

Human Destiny Foundation

Members of this organization believe that the destiny of humankind is to colonize our galaxy. They are alarmed by the fact that only a tiny fraction of Earth's 7 billion people show any interest in their dream. Mean-while, people are consuming resources that will be needed to build and fuel the fleet of starships for humanity's exodus. The HDF fears that humanity may be headed toward a final Malthusian equilibrium that consumes all of our productivity merely to sustain a tolerable standard of living for ten billion people more or less, thus leaving no resources to pursue *any* grand destiny, much less theirs. Members of HDF believe their destiny is to break this trend and direct humanity toward its "true" destiny.

Motivation for star travel requires a philosophic outlook. It is also philanthropic in the sense that the people who pay the bills reap no tangible benefit during their lifetime; they don't even satisfy their curiosity about the destination. Their motivation lies at the very pinnacle of Maslow's hierarchy of human needs.[65] People who work hard for subsistence never reach that level. This is HDF's major concern. They fear that our civilization will regress to some ultimate stable condition in which people are crowded, resources are scarce, standard of living barely tolerable, and star travel is merely a remote dream that recedes ever farther from realization.

Thus HDF wants prosperity above all and presumes that this requires a great decline in human population, especially people whose yearning never goes beyond simple creature comforts. This requisite differs little from those of the STR and SES. It evokes much the same hazardous untested depopulation schemes we've already seen in this chapter. Now you, dear reader, may conjure up an ending in which HDF devises a depopulation scheme, but something goes awry leading to the collapse of civilization or extinction of the human race.

2.4 Nanotechnology

Nanotech is the manipulation of matter on an atomic and molecular scale. By definition nanotech involves distances on the scale of 1 to 100 nanometers. One nanometer is the length of about 4 or 5 carbon atoms in a row depending on the kind of chemical bond between them. Quantum effects are observable at the short end of the nanometer scale, which will lead to novel inventions. Various new devices such as the scanning tunneling microscope and techniques such as fabrication of nanotubes and nanowires suggest that we are approaching an era of molecular manufacturing in which devices can be built by stacking molecules precisely where we want them. This will work wonders for making strong materials that exhibit the full strength of molecular bonds since they will no longer be weakened by defects, crystalline boundaries, and dislocations. Nanotech will give a big boost to miniaturization. Tiny machines will be feasible with gears and wheels in the nanometer to micrometer range.

Nanotech will endanger human life simply by enhancing other advanced technologies that are already dangerous. For example, our list above includes artificial life, artificial intelligence, and robotics. Suppose somebody living across town wants to kill you. He connects his computer to his desktop nanofabricator and downloads a program that makes several mosquito-bots. Then he chooses a lethal liquid and fabricates a tiny vial of the toxin. Perhaps he does this by rearranging groups of atoms in some related harmless substance. (Removal of one CH_2 group from harmless ethanol makes deadly methanol.) The mosquitoes suck in the toxin to load their stingers. Finally, your adversary gives them your address and photograph and sends them on their way.

Care to assassinate a president? Sometime in the next few decades the world may confront a major crime wave dominated by high-tech schemes using remote control. Futurist Michael Anissimov has discussed these possibilities.[66]

Martin Rees suggests that the “least bad” way to survive in such a world is to submit to intrusive government surveillance. 1 To preclude tyranny, surveillance must work in both directions with public sousveillance of government. David Brin wrote a book on this subject, *The Transparent Society.*[67] The idea that all citizens will soon have the tools with which they can watch each other and keep themselves accountable for their actions. This is called *participatory panopticon*. In the US a public outcry has questioned the National Security Agency’s domestic surveillance program, but that level of intrusion is minor compared to the sort that Rees’ suggestion would require. However, one can grow accustomed to intrusive surveillance, which eventually feels like a normal way of life. For example, enlisted military personnel submit to surprise inspections of their personal belongings.

A report by Robert A. Freitas[68] describes the dangers of molecular manufacturing (MM). A link in his first figure caption brings up a delightful animation of a nanofactory. He discusses a concept called grey goo, an infestation of nanobots, which appears in Section 2.5 below. Freitas argues persuasively that attempts to forbid MM would make the world more dangerous because it would fail to stop irresponsible development but would inhibit the good guys from developing defenses.

He discusses the need for regulation. The degree of control should vary with the degree of danger just as it does for other hazards. Drugs for example: off-the-shelf drugs like aspirin are lightly regulated, prescription drugs are heavily regulated, while addictive narcotics are banned.

2.5 Robotic infestation

Future applications for robots will include many that require vast numbers of tiny robots. In agriculture they will replace insecticides by picking pests individually off plants and trees. In orchards robo-crows will ward off birds trying to peck the fruit. Flying micro-robots will control mosquitoes by patrolling marshes and killing their eggs and larvae. They will seek out the small obscure places where mosquitoes breed, many of them things that collect rainwater such as puddles, buckets and bowls strewn about, abandoned tires, and so on.

Bigger swimming robots will exterminate invasive fish such as the Nile perch that has devastated Lake Victoria. An army of walking robots will clear kudzu out of southeastern US. Perhaps flying robots will rid Australia of invasive pests such as rabbits and cane toads. People have sometimes imported invasive species to control some pest with unpredictable results, sometimes disastrous. However, robotic pest control will be safe as long as the robots do not reproduce. When a problem occurs, one can simply stop production until the problem is fixed.

We have already met the lethal mosquito-bot. Think what a military aggressor can do with a few million of them. They may prefer to use non-lethal injections that sicken their adversary into submission. Or if they want to depopulate a big area, they can send robo-locusts to devour the crops. Clearly various terrorists, conspirators, and fanatics will want to unleash swarms of robots for their own malign purposes.

As the market for small robots grows, manufacturers will reduce shipping costs by building regional factories. Then as the number of regions grows, the manufacturer will build a master factory that produces automated regional factories. Perhaps this trend will continue until the master factory turns out regional factories that build portable factories that mass produce micro-robots numbering in the billions.

An alternative is to make a robot that mimics nature by replicating itself. However, no sane robot manufacturer working for profit would make a self-replicator on their own because their market vanishes the moment their customers start giving away surplus units (just as people give away surplus kittens). Besides, the result is inefficient because every unit must carry around a complete factory as part of its body even when there is insufficient material available for a new replica or no niche in which it can thrive.

Hobbyists will make robots that replicate themselves in a controlled environment by going to a stockroom and getting the parts they need, but this kind is not threatening. The real threat is something that can forage for its needs in the wild, but the R&D to make these self-replicators would be extremely expensive. This won't stop a billionaire hobbyist. For this and many other reasons, modern growth of extreme private wealth is a serious threat to humanity as discussed in Section 2.7.1 below.

No responsible agency would develop and unleash foraging self-replicators because they would lose control of them. That would be like importing an exotic species and releasing it in the wild. As invasive plants and animals have demonstrated, their numbers multiply and may lead to disaster. A robotic self-replicator might evolve (in the Darwinian sense) into a destructive pest like the locust or something worse. Governments will likely forbid self-replication by law.

However, from the terrorist's viewpoint, this disaster is just what he wants. The alternative, factories making factories, is too plodding and might give defenses a fighting chance. So the choices seem clear: terrorists want self-replicators; legitimate users want factories making factories. Terrorists will be disinclined to fund the huge amount of research and development required to make a self-replicator. For example, the terrorists of September 11, 2001 did not develop special aircraft optimized to destroy buildings. They simply hijacked craft that were readily available. Therefore, terrorists will most likely reject robotic infestation in favor of something more affordable and diabolical, perhaps a biological infestation aggravated by genetic engineering.

Eric Drexler, guru of nanotech, introduced a concept called *grey goo*, a name he now regrets. This would be a colony of nanobots that grows out of control by eating biomass just to make copies of themselves, a scenario called *ecophagy* (eating the environment).[69] Eventually the bots become a dense grey coating that covers nearly everything while expanding at its boundaries until the land is reduced to goo feces.[70] This idea spread out of control. Of course, how can anyone resist bandying such cool words as “grey goo” and “ecophagy”?

There is no reason to think that nanometers would be the optimum size for an omnivorous self-replicating devastator; it might be anything from a micrometer to something the size of a crow. Nature had billions of years to create such an animal, but barring undiscovered fossils, the closest she produced is swarming locusts. Various species have sizes like grasshoppers mostly in the range of a few centimeters. The biggest known swarm of locusts covered 500,000 km^2, comprising 12 trillion insects and weighing 27 million tons![71] This is equivalent to 54 grams/$meter^2$ over a 700 km square. More typical swarms are on the order of 100 billion insects.

No doubt some academic group will go beyond hobbyists and explore the limits of self-replication. What about the robot’s brain? Will it fabricate an integrated circuit from readily available feedstock, or will it be limited to standard IC chips from the stockroom? The brain may be the hardest part to replicate in a way that resembles nature.

For the rare roboticist who pursues self-replication in a harsher environment, nature offers a unique biological model, the planarian flatworm.[72] Most species live in freshwater, but some in salt water or on land. Lengths vary from 3 to 50 mm long, but tropical giant species grow to 60 cm. They reproduce both sexually and by fission. The latter is of interest here. The worm breaks in half, and the front end grows a new rear while the rear end grows a new front. Cutting a worm in pieces yields the same result.

The robotic version needs a "machine shop" to build the missing half after fission. This "shop" should be in the middle where it is most convenient to make an adjoining copy of itself. Then fission occurs between the two "shops." Each half then has a shop at the severed end where it needs to rebuild its missing half. At the time of fission, each half must already have building materials in storage. When regeneration is complete, the robot must forage to replace the materials used.

Reproductive models that are more complex than the planarian are too complicated for our robots. Any sort of nesting behavior, nurturing the young, foraging to feed them, and so forth are natural behaviors adapted to local environments and may have coevolved over many centuries with enemies and/or symbionts. Successful robotic self-replication must keep it simple as the planarian does.

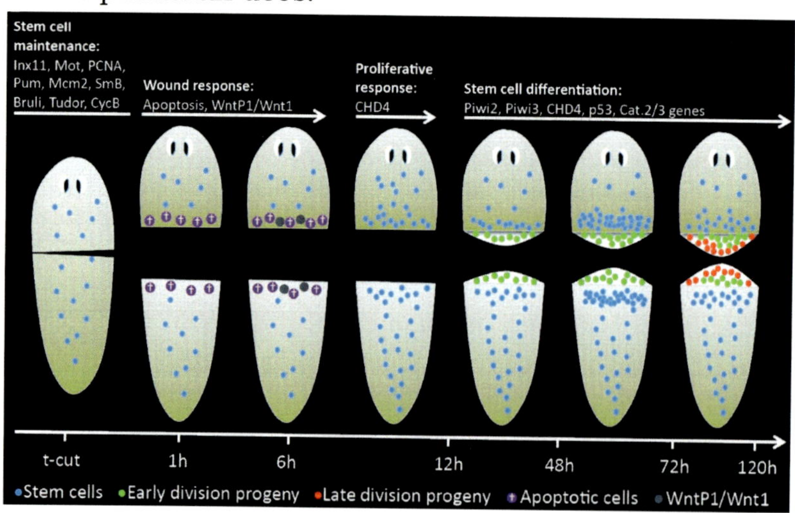

Planarian flatworm regeneration

2.6 Marine ecophagy

The amount of carbon in compounds produced by photosynthesis is called *primary production.* For the Earth it is 56.4 gigatonnes per year on land and 48.5 Gt/yr in the oceans. These are nearly equal. The loss of either one would cause mass starvation and would devastate the Earth with excessive carbon dioxide. As noted earlier, it was the picoplankton Cyanobacteria that gave us atmospheric oxygen billions of years ago in the Great Oxygenation Event, GOE. This was a switch from one fairly stable state to another. The prospect of switching back might be particularly attractive to someone seeking to destroy humanity because GOE has already demonstrated the switch in one direction.

Conspirators would choose marine ecophagy over land for many reasons. The amount of biomass on land is about a thousand times as much as the marine biomass despite the nearly equal primary production. If we limit ecophagy to phytomass (excluding zoomass) then land has 500 GtC compared to 200 MtC in the oceans, a ratio of 2,500. That's because land has big standing stocks such as tree trunks and roots. By contrast, nearly all the marine phytomass is being eaten all the time. Hence, marine ecophagy can devour the plant life by eating only a tiny fraction of the biomass that land ecophagy would have to eat, in effect a reversal of the GOE.

Other factors also favor aquatic ecophagy over land. The uniformity of seawater and lack of temperature extremes implies that fewer species of foragers are needed to do the job. Locomotion is simpler. The foragers need only swim; no need to cope with obstacles on land such as rivers, mountains, highways, nor to hide from people intent on destroying them. The foragers would float freely like plankton, only enough propulsion to scoop up their food and to adjust their depth for maximum forage.

Marine amphipod appendage
Feather-like setae serve as a plankton net.
The "arm" is around 0.8mm long.
Technique: Confocal microscopy
Dr. Igor Siwanowicz
HHMI Janelia Farm Research Campus, Ashburn, Virginia

Humans are masters of the land, where we would detect ecophagy early, fight the infestation furiously and quite possibly win. By contrast, there are great ocean areas that lack any sort of surveillance or instrumentation that would detect suspicious activity. These arguments are so compelling that we should dismiss entirely any distractions about ecophagy on land and focus our attention on the threat at sea.

Phytoplankton lie at the base of the marine food chain. Creatures that eat them range from millimeter-sized zooplankton to Baleen whales. Krill are shrimp-like crustaceans (zooplankton) about 5 centimeters long weighing about one gram. Antarctic krill are among the largest of 85 known species. Estimates of their mass range from 125 million tons to 6 billion tons in the waters around Antarctica, one of the world's most massive species comparable to the mass of all humans.[73, 74] They graze on phytoplankton at the bottom of the food chain making them in effect the fuel that runs the engine of the Earth's marine ecosystems.

Krill are a possible target for a conspiracy to upset the biosphere. Using techniques of genetic engineering, conspirators might create particularly voracious varieties of krill that deplete the phytoplankton. If they could devour absolutely all of it, this would reverse the GOE, but of course there will always be survivors somewhere. The question is whether mutant krill can cause an event big enough to threaten human life, either a transient event or a shift in the equilibrium state.

Antarctic krill
Wikimedia commons

This scenario would require careful analysis because there is a mitigating effect: the amount of phytomass is limited less by grazing than by nutrients, especially nitrogen, iron, and phosphorus. We know this because algae bloom where rainwater carries fertilizer into the sea. Moreover, iron sprinkled on blue seawater causes a bloom,[75] which turns it green. Thus rapid grazing by mutant krill would leave more nutrients and allows phytoplankton to reproduce faster.

2.7 Other man-made hazards

Hazards that are man-made or facilitated by human activity include ...

- genetic engineering & artificial life (viruses, microbes)
- deforestation
- environmental toxin
- man-made component of climate change
- pandemic aggravated by human activity and overpopulation
- nuclear war, nuclear winter
- doomsday bomb (huge hydrogen or cobalt)
- nanotechnology
- ill-advised geoengineering
- high-energy physics (Large Hadron Collider)
- miscellany, to be discussed.

Most of these hazards are byproducts of normal progress in science, technology, and industry. However, they are also tools that terrorists, conspirators, and fanatics can employ for their nefarious goals. Bill Gates has emphasized the risk of pandemic in a speech he gave in February 2017 at the annual Munich Security Conference.[76] Gates thinks that we are due for an apocalyptic sickness on the scale of the Spanish Influenza in 1918 that killed 50 million people.

Most hazards on the list above are simply the "usual suspects" that other scholars have studied and written about. No need to rehash them all; however, I have variants and unconventional views about some of them, which follow in the remaining sections of this chapter.

2.7.1 Latent killer

A fatal contagion has a very long incubation period, as do BSE (bovine spongiform encephalopathy) and AIDS (acquired immune deficiency syndrome). By the time its symptoms appear, air/sea travel already will have carried it to tiny populated islands and remote outposts. Wherever the epidemic strikes, it infects everybody before any symptoms appear, and by then it is too late for quarantine. Incidentally, if a microbe kills too quickly, its victims have little time to infect others. Thus, latency enhances the microbe's reproduction, and so natural selection reinforces this trait. Although diseases kill individuals, they rarely kill their host species. That would detract from the microbe's reproduction. Therefore, the killer probably will not evolve naturally. But genetic engineers can make it happen either by accident or on purpose. A lone mad scientist is not out of the question.

Precedent: BSE can lie dormant for decades.

Survivors: possibly the remotest islanders.

2.7.2 Contraception

A genetically engineered virus or bacterium makes women permanently infertile. When they have all the children they want, they deliberately infect themselves. This may be the perfect solution to overpopulation in pronatalist traditional societies because wives need not tell their husbands nor use devices or pills that he might discover. Organizations that promote family planning make the virus available worldwide. Eventually the virus mutates and becomes contagious. Nobody suspects anything until someone notices a loss of sales for maternity merchandise. By then, the mutant variety has spread worldwide.

Precedent: Researchers at Washington University used genetically modified salmonella bacteria to produce harmless, temporary infections able to act as contraceptives. Infected women were infertile for months.

Survivors: communal religious groups with minimal outside contact, e.g. Hutterites; and women who happen to have been isolated while the contagion spread undetected and then go into quarantine following the discovery. Ultimately a vaccination or other treatment will probably be developed. Meanwhile, society's adaptation will depend on many things: Are juvenile girls vulnerable? Infants? Are males carriers?

2.7.3 Business as usual

A man-made hazard need not be high-tech to pose a catastrophic threat. Proliferation of ordinary industrial activity can also be lethal. Let us review a scenario in my book *Apocalypse When?*,[10] on pages 97–8, **mutant phytoplankton**. Some plankton are toxic. They bloom in shallow water where fish and shellfish ingest the toxin and many die. People eat the seafood and some of them die too. Especially well known are toxic red blooms of certain dinoflagellates, the so-called *red tides*.

This toxin is in the bodies of the plankton, but suppose a mutant plankton produces toxic vapor that evaporates into the atmosphere. By the time the source is identified, it would most likely have spread beyond control. If the mutant variety prospers and overpowers competing species, it could poison the entire atmosphere. This would be doomsday because we cannot treat the entire surface of the world's oceans with herbicide.

Red tide
Courtesy of National Institute of Water and Atmospheric Research, New Zealand

Although unlikely, this scenario is not as far-fetched as it may seem because plankton have already dramatically altered our atmosphere. About 2.4 billion years ago oceanic cyanobacteria (blue-green algae) converted Earth's atmosphere of carbon dioxide into the air we breathe today in the so-called *Great Oxygenation Event* (GOE), which killed off former anoxic life forms.[77]

Compare this scenario with one in which a terrestrial plant emits toxic vapor. Technicians wearing gas masks would quickly trace the toxin to its source and eradicate it. Since we are land animals; we know what's going on here and have the means to control it. The worst mutant on land might be one that produces wind blown seeds that spread like dandelion or tumbleweed.

So what could cause this mutation? If it were a natural event, it would have happened long ago since nature has had billions of years to discover it. (Perhaps it did happen, and our species is among the survivors.) Human activity can cause this mutation either by accident or deliberately by a rogue genetic engineer. Since pollution is known to cause mutations, a discharge of waste bio-chemicals into the ocean might do it. If the source is detected very quickly, we might exterminate the mutant with herbicide or a deliberate oil spill. But this is unlikely in ordinary coastal water that is not continually sampled or otherwise monitored for suspicious activity. Doomsday follows if currents and wind-driven turbulence diffuse the mutant beyond limits of containment and our whole atmosphere becomes toxic.

Precedent: the great oxygenation event, toxic dinoflagellates.

Survivors: none.

2.7.4 Outrageous private wealth

Forbes magazine publishes an annual report on the 400 richest Americans. In 2006 for the first time, all 400 were billionaires. In 2004 there were 313 billionaires, compared to 262 in 2003. This is not merely an artifact of inflation. As Fig. 3 shows, the wealthiest 0.01% quadrupled their share of the total between 1980 and 2012. At the rate private fortunes are accruing, there will be trillionaires before long. Will all of them be sane? What about their heirs? Will the U.S. Federal Bureau of Investigation or any other intelligence agency keep tabs on them?

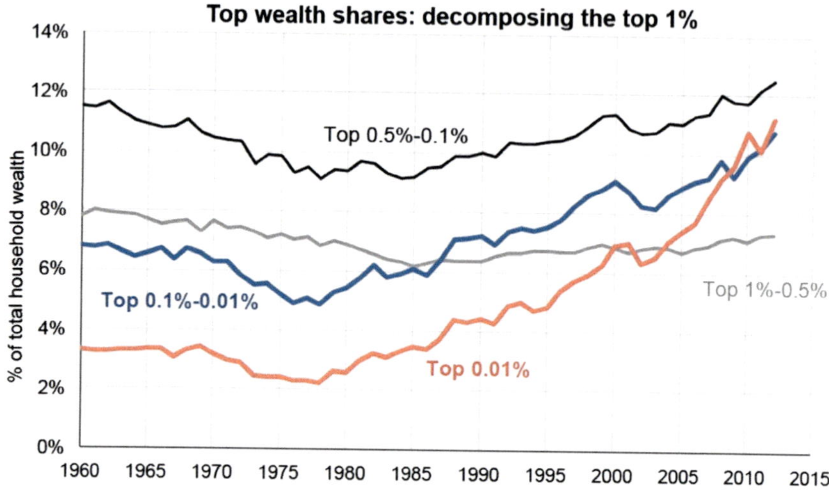

Fig. 3. Wealth inequality in the United States: fraction held by the wealthiest[78]

My first book (*AW* p. 105) gave one example of a crazy multimillionaire who was convicted of murder, John E. du Pont, one of many heirs to the eponymous chemical company. Now another example is in the news, an heir to some hundreds of millions. He is Robert Alan Durst, currently charged with first-degree murder, and the probable killer of three. His life history of crime and eccentric behavior is incredibly complex[79] and currently under investigation.

Crazies have committed horrendous, senseless crimes and claimed that they acted on orders from God. Trillionaires are not immune to such delusions. If and when a trillionaire imagines God's command to end the human race, he may have the will and the power to succeed. Any one trillionaire would be able to buy weapons of mass destruction. He could purchase a nation, put its leaders on his payroll, rewrite its laws, and take its seat in the United Nations, perhaps the Security Council.

He can build secret laboratories and hire scientists and technicians most of whom would work under some pretext and be unaware of their employer's true motives. A deranged trillionaire may create some infestation (probably biological) that reproduces exponentially until it exterminates or decimates the human race. Among the world's 200 nations there are surely a few where corrupt officials can be bribed to allow this scourge to be developed in secret.

2.7.5 Geoengineering

Geoengineering spreads large quantities of some feedstock either in the atmosphere or ocean to adjust the climate or biosphere. This is risky even when designed by the most qualified scientists in the field since Earth is too complex to be fully predictable.

Moreover, geoingineering has a dependency problem: once begun, the entire world adapts to the new environment. So what happens if it must be discontinued due to some unforeseen side effect? Or if it exhausts the supply of feedstock?

A multibillionaire undertakes his own solution to global warming. After minimal research and maximal hunch, he decides to seed the stratosphere with an aerosol that he alone has formulated. He hires a huge fleet of high-altitude jets and proceeds to spray over international waters beyond the jurisdiction of any nation. This happens without any consensus among scientists or approval of any form.

You may continue this story as you wish with any number of climate disasters.

Precedent: A hundred tonnes of iron sulfate were dumped off the coast of British Columbia to fertilize a phytoplankton bloom,[80] which was illegal and arguably irresponsible.

Survivors: Unknown. A severe climate change might have no survivor.

2.7.6 Global warming mixed with politics

Two climate monitoring stations suffer simultaneous failures that mask an Orange Alert. By the time the trouble is fixed, it has become a Red Alert. Coincidentally there is protracted tension between industrial nations and the underdeveloped world. Leaders in four populous nations assert themselves by refusing to respond to the Red Alert because that would be seen as cooperation with the industrial world. They claim the alert is a political ruse and refuse to shut down their national consumption of fossil fuel. Before the United Nations can enforce the Climate Treaty, it is too late.

Peter Ward has found evidence that global warming was responsible for some of the major mass extinctions in Earth's past,[59] in particular the greatest of all, the Permian/Triassic (P/T) extinction in which 90% of land species vanished. Normally vertical circulation of seawater carries oxygen to the sea floor. This so-called thermohaline circulation results from the densest seawater sinking to the bottom, density being determined by temperature (thermo-) and salinity (-haline). However, global warming can raise sea temperature to a point where this circulation fails. Anoxic deep water then supports bacteria that turn the water black and emit hydrogen sulfide (H_2S). This gas is poisonous to most animals including humans and also removes ozone from the upper atmosphere, which protects us from ultraviolet sunlight. Ward argues that atmospheric concentration of H_2S has reached toxic levels several times during the history of life on Earth. It also turns the sky green, hence the title of his book, *Under a Green Sky*.

2.7.7 High-energy physics

Some folks express concern that high-energy particle physics might somehow create tiny black holes, or rip the fabric of space-time, or somehow cause an instant end to our universe. The American Institute of Physics has formally looked into this and reported that there is no risk. In particular, nature has long been making particle collisions that are more energetic than any that man can hope to make now or in the foreseeable future. What residual doubt may remain is further reduced by the fact that the Large Hadron Collider in Geneva has successfully produced the Higgs Boson, its first big goal, without incident or cause for alarm.

2.7.8 Nuclear war, nuclear winter

We all know the enormous devastation nuclear war can wreak. However, for the purpose of this book we have defined catastrophic risk as something akin to the collapse of civilization or worse. In nuclear war all the weapons and all their targets are in the Northern Hemisphere. To the south, air circulation follows latitudinal bands. Populated regions of the far south, New Zealand's South Island, Tasmania, Tierra del Fuego, and the Falkland Islands are all isolated from fallout and nuclear winter by two so-called Hadley cells of air circulation, and all these areas would survive the worst war and perpetuate civilization.

However, nuclear terrorism is something else. The perpetrators could transport bombs and spread them more or less equally around the globe. Your everyday terrorists probably lack the means to acquire and smuggle nukes since they are tracked more carefully than your everyday contraband, but a super sophisticated misanthrope is always a possibility.

2.7.9 Hypercoherence

In about 1991 I was touring National Parks in southern Utah (which I highly recommend). Late one afternoon I went off the road into some gravel to make a U-turn; there a big nail punctured my tire. Someone nearby let me use their telephone to call for help. (Remember, no cell phones in 1991.) By the time we were mobile again it was too late to move on, so we looked for local lodging. The motels in this small town were full, so we made a few inquiries and found a B&B, where the landlady took pity and fixed us a late supper.

Fast-forward to 2014 when we toured that area again. Remembering the 1991 experience, we decided to forego reservations for lodging because we wanted flexibility to modify our plans. All went well until Columbus Day, a three-day weekend. Using iPhones to search the Internet, we soon learned that *every* last room was booked, and so we were forced to take a long detour. This happened because modern technology gave potential tourists the ability to seek out the very last room. In earlier times, some would have given up the search and stayed home, thus leaving some resilience in a system that has now become rigid.

Arthur Demarest, an anthropologist at Vanderbilt University calls this condition *hypercoherence*.[81] He has studied the collapse of ancient civilizations and found that they often fell soon after they reached their apex of achievement and prosperity, just where we are now. He also says,

> Hypercoherence is one of the most dangerous threats to the long-term survival of our civilization. Hypercoherence is the close efficient linkage of all parts of the world economic, communication and transport systems. It has been crucial in the spread of great innovations, the rise of world wealth, and even the dissemination of democratic concepts and ethical values and the defeat of oppressive regimes.
>
> However, this strength is ... one of the most common symptoms of impending collapse. Perturbations, even small ones, immediately radiate throughout the entire system. Today there are few, if any, refuges against international crises of any kind. Thus, our brilliant communication, information, and transport systems, which will be remembered as the hallmark of our age, are also a point of great fragility.

A good example of hypercoherence is the electric power system. The Northeast blackout of 2003 affected 55 million people in Canada and U.S. Some power was restored 7 hours later, but the typical duration was about 2 days. Imagine trying to explain this possibility to Thomas Edison in 1882 when he switched on electricity to 59 customers in lower Manhattan.

Back to Arthur Demarest, let us digress a bit on his view of leadership during the process of collapse:

> Leaders may recognize that they are not addressing the real problems, but they rationalize their actions with the argument that they must first politically survive in order to later address the hard problems and sacrifices. Of course, they usually don't ever actually get around to addressing the fundamental problems later, either because they don't make it through the initial crisis or because, even later, they are not willing to risk sacrificing their own position (or "career") with needed measures that usually require tough sacrifices by the population.

Sound familiar?

2.7.10 Zombies

The vast majority of animal zombies are insects,[82] but there are exceptions that infect mammals. The parasite *Toxoplasma gondii* causes rodents to lose their instinctive fear of cats and be mildly attracted by the odor of cats.[83] This enables the parasite to complete its life cycle in the cat's gut, the only place it can sexually reproduce.

It is most unlikely that a purely natural process will produce human zombies since nature has already had 2,000 centuries to do so, and there is no evidence that it has happened. However, the zealots and mad scientists in our future may produce human zombies with the tools of artificial biology. They may appear perfectly normal until they suddenly behave in some deadly way, and they may be contagious.

2.7.11 Threats with stories

Throughout human history telling stories about disasters has saved myriad individuals and tribes because stories help us understand which of the myriad possible threats are actually plausible. No doubt this has reinforced our instinct for storytelling. Efforts to compose disaster stories are a good way to fill out a list of overlooked hazards.

Brief examples of story-like threats appear above. The subsection *Global warming mixed with politics* adumbrates a story. *Hypercoherence* contains a brief account of my own experience. *Outrageous private wealth* invites a story about a mad trillionaire. *Mutant phytoplankton* suggests a thriller about a desperate effort to contain a mutant species as it diffuses into open ocean. The subsection *Geoengineering* invites a story about an organization like Greenpeace desperately trying to impede a rogue geoengineer operating in international waters. Each of the three fictional organizations under *Zealotry* could be the basis of a story. The world needs books full of brief short stories like these to identify hazards that we have overlooked.

Chapter 3. How to save the human race

My main recommendation is to develop and install artificial intelligence that serves as humanity's supervisor and caretaker, an AI Nanny. However, that may not happen. An authority may intervene, or the Nanny may not be ready in time. Thus the subject of this chapter is what else we can do.

Imagine that Earth had been bombarded by a series of medium-sized bolides starting about 66 million years ago. Let's say average interval between strikes was a few thousand years. Many of these impacts would have killed some dinosaurs, sometimes whole species. However, as survivors bred with survivors, they would have adapted to the bolide-ridden environment. Then a million years later many species would have survived the big impact at Chicxulub. But that's not what happened; the big one hit first, and the rest is history.

This **dinosaur paradigm** now applies to the human race. We are exposed to climate change and all the man-made hazards discussed in Chapter 2, which proliferate at an accelerating pace. Eventually a major catastrophe will strike. Like the dinosaurs, much depends on the magnitude of the first instance.

Suppose it kills billions and destroys civilization, but millions residing in remote locations survive and rebuild. All high-tech hazards will be destroyed or forgotten, so the residual risk of extinction will be minuscule. Atmospheric carbon dioxide will return to its normal concentration, nature will reclaim the tropics, and so on. It may not be a happy time, especially if despots rule the survivors, but at least our environment will recover and the human race will survive. Wiser for the experience, survivors and their offspring are unlikely to make a similar mistake, and so humankind may safely rebuild to fulfill its destiny, perhaps to colonize our galaxy.

A lesser first catastrophe may kill or disable a billion people more or less and displace or impoverish another billion. Frightened survivors then accept oppressive government regulation, taxation, and intrusive surveillance to ensure this never happens again. So even though civilization survives, including hazardous high tech, this event may suffice to save humanity from extinction for the few centuries of interest here. In the distant future memory of the event will fade into ancient history, and earthlings become vulnerable again. But hopefully by that time humans will have redundant colonies somewhere beyond Earth, and so our species will be safe again. *The most dangerous time is now, a critical period after technology has created the hazards, but before it provides habitats for escape.*

However, the first catastrophe may be the big one, the species killer. Like dinosaurs humanity may be caught unprepared, because without a precursory event people will not accept intrusive government oversight that might forestall the big one.

An obvious precaution is to establish a number of survival colonies in a variety of locations that offer protection from various hazards. Traditional survivalists,[84] aka doomsday preppers, generally assume that disaster will pass, and in its aftermath they will find other survivors to join in restoring a society. Our colonies must be more sophisticated. We should assume that other survivors may not exist, or if they do, colonists have no transport to join the others even if they are in contact by radio and know each others location.

This means that each colony needs enough members to ensure genetic diversity and thus comprise a viable breeding stock in isolation. Certain ethnic groups are known to suffer from too much inbreeding, well known examples being the Amish and Ashkenazi Jews.

An extreme example of a small group that manages to survive is the inhabitants of the isolated islands of Tristan da Cunha (koon-yah) in the far South Atlantic[85]. Their original population was 8 men and 7 women who arrived at various times in the 19th century. A Russian appeared shortly after 1900, and 4 Englishmen in 1963. Their health problems are relatively few, high incidence of asthma and glaucoma. Fortunately the original inhabitants supplied great genetic diversity having come from Europe, Africa, and the Orient.

For our purposes it will be reasonable to require a minimum of about 100 colonists.[86] Of course it will help greatly if they are racially diverse and screened for genetic disease. Fewer colonists will suffice if they are mostly women supplied with frozen semen from a variety of donors.

Frozen semen is normally stored in vials suspended in liquid nitrogen inside a Dewar flask. There is no time limit for storing it; one sample stored for 21 years produced a healthy boy.[87] However, even the best flasks evaporate almost 2% per day, and so storage for years requires means for making liquid nitrogen from air.

3.1 Space habitat

We have been assuming a guesstimated 5 centuries as the crucial time before earthlings develop a redundant habitat in space. One good way to improve our long-term survival prospects would be to shorten that delay. The moon is not a good place to put that habitat. It is biologically hostile due to temperature extremes, long nights, and adverse effects of low gravity. Its hard vacuum exposes humans to solar flares, tiny meteors, and other radiation. However, the moon may play an important role in timely development of a space habitat, a role that physicist Philip Metzger is promoting.

Metzger participated in a NASA expedition to a barren region on Mauna Kea in Hawaii. Experiments there convinced him that it is feasible to initiate a robotic industrial revolution on the moon using mostly lunar resources and thereby avoid the enormous expense of hauling material from Earth.[88] Metzger and his coauthors estimate that the seed can be planted on the moon with a payload of only 12 tonnes during a period of 20 years. The equipment can be teleoperated from Earth during its early phases (round trip communication delay = 2.5 seconds) with the intent of eventual full autonomy and artificial intelligence on the moon.

During the first phase robots will be preoccupied with their own "life support," setting up solar panels, finding resources, extracting minerals from regolith, making spare parts with 3D printers, and the like. Once established, they can build crude machine shops that will eventually evolve into good machine shops in a process conceptually similar to the industrial revolution on Earth but with numerous practical differences. Due to modern knowledge the lunar revolution will proceed much faster than the original industrial revolution. In some ways it will bc more difficult than the original. For example, we earthlings are accustomed to abundant water, and so we wash things in water that we discard, but on the moon, water will be strictly conserved. On Earth we take wet chemistry for granted, but on the moon it will be plagued by evaporation and strict conservation.

Other processes will be easier on the moon. Everything will be light weight, and structures for shade need not withstand wind. Anything that requires a vacuum, such as vapor deposition of thin films can be open to the vacuum of space. Very light-weight objects need not be manufactured on the moon because they can be imported from Earth in abundance. One example is curved mirrors to concentrate sunlight. They will be light because the surface accuracy need be no more accurate that the angular radius of the sun, a quarter of a degree in angle. They will replace the massive furnaces we use in earthly industrial processes.

Eventually lunar robots develop high tech and replicate more robots. However, they need not fabricate their own silicon chips for ICs and digital memories, at least not at first. Chips are so small that they can be imported from Earth both for computers and robot brains.

A NASA lunar base concept with a mass driver (the long structure that extends toward the horizon) for space launches
Wikipedia, public domain

After many years of exponential expansion the lunar infrastructure will be ready to build spaceships and space habitats for humans. Ultimately it will extend into the asteroid belt and build starships.

A strong candidate for space habitats is O'Neill's cylinder.[89,90,91] It is a cylindrical spaceship spinning about its axis to provide artificial gravity for a human colony living on the curved inside wall. Normally cylinders will be built in counter-rotating pairs so that the net angular momentum is zero. This facilitates initially revving the pair up to speed: the motor on either cylinder that torques the other produces an equal but opposite reaction torque on itself; in other words, torque need not be external to the cylinders. Moreover, net zero angular momentum facilitates controlling the pair's attitude toward the sun throughout its solar orbit.

Artist's depiction of an O'Neill pair
Wikipedia, public domain

Interior view, showing land and window stripes
Wikipedia, public domain

Space habitats are not the only incentive for an industrial revolution on the moon. The benefits to astronomy would be revolutionary. Phased arrays of telescopes can achieve an aperture of a large fraction of the moon's diameter, 3.5 megameters. Suppose the array aperture is $A = 2.5 \times 10^6$ meters. At the wavelength of green light, 5×10^{-7} meters, the basic angular resolution would be

$$\text{angular res.} = \lambda/A = 2 \times 10^{-13} \text{ radian}$$

A light year is about 1.0×10^{16} meters, and so the linear resolution at stellar distances of 10 and 100 lt.yrs. would be 20 kilometers and 200 km., good enough to see exoplanets in great detail.

Of course realization will not happen smoothly. Rejection of direct light from the parent star must be nearly perfect. Moreover, when the angular resolution is this extreme, we will see disturbances we have never seen before, for example, effects of thermal expansion with a period of 28 days, and solar tides with a period of 14 days. Earth causes no tide on the moon because the moon does not rotate relative to Earth, but it may wobble enough to make a disturbance at this high resolution.

3.2 Earthbound refuges

The first space habitat will accommodate only a few earthlings, while the vast majority remain earthbound. A lucky few of those may find safe havens here near the surface. The safest of these require expensive preparations and government support, which means long delays to organize political support, contact government agencies, and persuade elected representatives. The opportunity to begin some of them may have already passed.

3.2.1 Nuclear submarines

Some members of the Lifeboat Foundation[92] have noted that submerged nuclear submarines are probably the safest refuges, vulnerable to nothing short of boiling ocean. US and Russia own most of them, but the UK, France, India, and China are also players. Retired missile launching submarines (SSBNs) would make ideal refuges because missile-launching tubes can be converted to store provisions for prolonged cruises. The size of the crew, >100, is just about right for a survival colony. Smaller attack submarines would be usable, but not optimum because a survival colony has no need for their speed and maneuverability. Sadly, retired US boats are dismantled and cut in pieces.[93] Some 150 to 170 Russian/Soviet boats have been removed from service and remain in varying conditions of disrepair.[94]

USS Michigan (SSBN-727), an Ohio-class Trident vessel in dry dock
(public domain)

In the US Navy, SSBNs currently on patrol belong to the Ohio class,[95] 18 of them now in service. Their displacement is 16,764 tonnes surfaced, length 170 meters, beam 13 m. Their crew is 15 officers and 140 sailors. Time at sea is limited only by food storage. Storage canisters to put in missile tubes can be roughly the same size as the missiles they replace, 24 tridents each 13 m. long, 2.11 m. in diameter, for a total storage volume of 1091 cubic meters = 1.1 million liters. Let's say that each person requires 2 liters of expendable supplies, mostly dried food, per day. (The average human stomach comfortably holds about 1 liter.) Then the 155 people on board need 310 liters each day, and so the full storage space lasts for 3500 days, almost ten years. Much of the food commercially available for emergency rations is advertised to last 25 years. The Navy plans to retire the Ohio class beginning in 2029, which gives us 13 years to persuade the Navy to maintain retired boats in a condition where they can be pressed into service on short notice, perhaps a few months.

In the 60-year history of nuclear ships[96] only one nuclear attack submarine has ever attacked an enemy: HMS Conqueror (S48) sank the Argentine cruiser General Belgrano during the 1982 Falklands War.[97] No SSBN has ever launched a missile in hostility. Thus, it may seem that the probability of needing SSBNs as survival habitats may exceed the probability of needing them to launch missiles, and indeed this is the case as we shall show.

Pretend for the moment that there had been 3 missile attacks in those 60 years. We would estimate the probability rate at 3/60 = 5% per year. Using that simple ratio in the real case of zero attacks would put the probability at 0%/year, which of course was not true sixty years ago and is not true now. There are other well known probability puzzles like this one that fail at the low end, the best known being Laplace's rule of succession described in Appendix A. So for a crude estimate of the probability of a submarine missile attack, assume that the probability was originally 50% for the 60-year period, but as events played out, there were by luck zero attacks rather than the one or two that might have happened. So let us estimate the probability rate as

$$50\%/60 \text{ years} = 0.8\%/\text{year}.$$

In Section 4.9 below we estimate that the current risk rate for civilization is 4.5%/year. Of course there are many possible scenarios for civilization's collapse, but it seems likely that SSBNs are effective survival habitats in most of them, in which case the relative importance of the two roles is simply the ratio of these two risk rates, namely 5.6. In other words, *the chance that SSBNs would "make history" as survival habitats is about six times greater than the chance they will "make history" as missile launch platforms.*

Of course strategic warriors will quickly point out that SSBNs serve as deterrents even if they never fire a missile in hostility. However, the deterrent role would be compromised very little if the boats were modified to serve both roles. Half the missile tubes (12) would be adequate deterrent leaving the other 12 for storing provisions. Or they could carry 8 missiles and 16 storage canisters. If our world were rational, navies should already be modifying their active SSBNs to serve both as warships and as survival habitats.

For obvious biological reasons, each crew of a survival habitat should be majority women. Scandinavian navies have long included women on their submarines; one of them is a commanding officer. However, these are small submarines that spend limited time at sea. The U.S. Navy has only recently added women officers to the crews of big SSBNs without any modification to the boats. (Officer's quarters offer more privacy than sailor's quarters have.) For the survivalist role, the crew should include a midwife and a medic with knowledge of pediatrics. A supply of frozen semen would improve genetic diversity in a post-apocalyptic aftermath. So, who has the chutzpah to propose this change to appropriate admirals and government officials? (I am an ex-naval officer, but reluctant to take on that chore.)

3.2.2 Space colony simulator

Someday a space agency may send astronauts to build a colony on Mars. NASA and other organizations are already making preparations by building structures to simulate an extraterrestrial environment so that proxy astronauts can practice building living quarters, greenhouses to raise crops and livestock, recycling water and sewage, and whatever else is required to operate a sustainable colony. Simulations include the round trip communications delay to Mars, which is 8.8 minutes when Earth and Mars are aligned on the same side of Sun, the so-called opposition[98] from the viewpoint of an earthbound observer. This delay extends to 42 minutes when Earth and Mars are aligned on opposite sides, so-called conjunction. The longest delays imply a need for on-site decision making, presumably by humans at the Mars site.

Simulation structures might serve a dual purpose as a refuge during an existential disaster,[99] but unlike submarines, the existing few are much too small to accommodate a genetically viable colony. This limitation is likely to remain. Even if we ultimately build a giant spaceship to take a hundred colonists to Mars, a much smaller group is adequate to simulate the problems they will encounter.

Preliminary projects of this sort have already begun. NASA is in the second phase of project HI-SEAS, in which three men and three women live at 8200 ft altitude in a thousand-square-foot dome built on Mauna Loa, Hawaii.[100] The acronym denotes Hawaii Space Exploration Analog and Simulation.[101]

Russia, China, and the European Space Agency conducted a joint experiment in psychosocial isolation called Mars-500 between 2007 and 2011 in Moscow.[102] It included a mockup spacecraft and living quarters, and such features as telemedicine and communication delays with the outside world up to 25 minutes. A private organization, the Mars Society,[103] is conducting its own simulation in the far Canadian arctic, Mars Arctic 365.[104]

3.2.3 Hydrothermal vent

In an extreme situation the entire Earth's surface may be toxic, too hot, or otherwise uninhabitable for centuries. Until we have a habitat in outer space, the only alternative is one undersea near natural sources of food and power. That would be hydrothermal vents in the sea floor[105] that eject hot water through cracks in the Earth's crust. They are found in great variety at all depths and many are biologically productive, but none have been studied as places to live with a source of food. Site surveys for human habitation would be a huge undertaking, but if there is no alternative, and if we have some years of advanced warning, then that will happen.

The first hydrothermal vent was discovered in 1976 on the Galápagos Rift at a depth of 2.5 km. Since then, more than 200 fields have been documented in great variety. If at first you don't find one to your liking, just keep looking. Perhaps the best known are black smokers,[106] which have sulfides dissolved in their outflow. As the stream mixes with cold ambient water, sulfides precipitate as black smoke and form huge black chimneys. Another type such as the "Lost City" near the mid-Atlantic ridge produces huge white carbonate chimneys.[107]

Areas around these vents are biologically productive. In many the light is so dim that the base of the food chain is not photosynthesis but rather chemosynthesis, based on chemicals dissolved in hot water coming from the vent. Fauna may include clams, limpets, shrimp, and giant tube worms. Surely some of these are edible, but we have no report from gastronomes. Crabs, fish, octopi, and eels inhabit some vent areas, but the species adapted to vents are very different from the familiar ones. Characteristic species differ somewhat in the Atlantic, Pacific, and Indian oceans.

Fauna at a hydrothermal vent
Courtesy of Stephen Low Productions[108]

What about vegetables? In the photic zone it is possible to filter phytoplankton from the water. Recall that Japanese cuisine includes sea vegetables. At deep vents the base of the food chain is chemosynthetic bacteria. They grow into a thick mat that other organisms graze on. Perhaps it is possible to process these mats for food with fiber and nutrients like those found in ordinary vegetables. If this seems disgusting, recall that staple foods in some parts of the world are naturally toxic until processed. Taro corms (like bulbs) must be cooked in water with a bit of baking soda to remove calcium oxalate,[109] and cassava (aka manioc or tapioca-root) must be processed to remove cyanide.[110] Finally, if there is no way to obtain vegetables, recall that Eskimos thrive on diet with hardly any vegetable matter.[111] Obviously, extensive site surveys and nutritional research would be required to make this habitat feasible.

Vents occur at all depths. (Iceland is essentially a vent above water.) The optimum is probably a compromise. For human adaptation to pressure we would like a shallow vent, and for ambient light we'd like it to be in the photic zone, which extends to about 200 meters in the clearest water. However, if global warming is what drives us to the sea floor, then we may need greater depth to stay cool. Cold water from the polar regions sinks and flows all the way to the tropics without warming more than a few degrees Celsius.

If our colony generates power by means of a heat engine such as a gas turbine, then we want the maximum temperature difference between the stream from the hydrothermal vent at T_2 and ambient water a few yards away where the gas condenses at T_1. The theoretical maximum efficiency of conversion from heat to mechanical energy, the so-called Carnot efficiency, is $1 - T_1/T_2$, where temperature is expressed in Kelvin (Celsius plus 273). This efficiency is very good in deep water where we may find vent outflow at 400 °C and ambient at 2 °C:

$$\text{Carnot efficiency } = 1 - \frac{275\,K}{673\,K} = 59\,\%$$

A sizable heat engine working with these temperatures can supply power for electric lighting and machinery for light industry as well as life-support equipment for fresh water, fresh air, and dehumidification. Temperature differences are usually much less in shallow water, but exceptions may be found if we just continue searching.

An underwater habitat normally takes fresh air from the surface by way of a hose.[112] This may or may not be feasible depending on the disaster scenario that forces us to the sea floor. If not, we can consider an air recycling system such as those used on submarines. These typically use electrolytic oxygen, scrubbers to remove carbon dioxide, and various filters to remove other contaminants. Trouble is, these systems make no special effort to conserve energy, especially on a submarine with nuclear power. This might overtax a power system based on a modest hydrothermal vent.

The habitat would be a craft filled with artificial air at ambient pressure having a moon pool in the bottom of the hull where workers can dive into the water or descend a ladder to the seafloor.[113,114] From there they have easy access to the nearby hydrothermal vent and all the power equipment and wildlife around it.

Vents occur at cracks in the Earth's crust, and the major deep-sea vent fields occur where tectonic plates meet. Consequently, the location of a vent can drift and its intensity can change when earthquakes occur. For example, a small quake off the coast of Washington caused a nearby vent system to pump out ten times its normal flow of hot water.[115]

A site survey to find the best vent for a survival colony would be a huge project far beyond the scope of this treatise. The existing literature is not much help because each author is interested in the features that pertain to his specialty, not all the features that would affect him if he were planning to live there. The geologists care about the fault and hot rocks that underlie the vent, biologists are interested in the species that live there, and somebody planning a power plant cares about the water temperatures and the volumetric flow rate. For example, one of the few papers on power generation shows the feasibility of an electric generator at vents in the Gulf of California where they could power desalination plants to irrigate the nearby Mexican desert,[116] but the author tells us nothing that bears on the feasibility of a habitat at this site.

3.3 A Grim Choice

Consider a big statistical sample of equally likely futures for the crucial century in which we live. According to my calculations summarized in Chapter 4 below, roughly half of these futures end in extinction and half in long-term survival; see Fig. 24 in Section 4.10 below. However, in the surviving half, almost every future includes a collapse of civilization. This collapse is what saves us by destroying man-made hazards that would otherwise lead to extinction. This is like the dinosaur paradigm: if the greater disaster strikes first, we are dead; if the lesser strikes first, it immunizes us.

Meanwhile, we are living in the present not knowing which of these futures will transpire. Suppose that threats to civilization worsen to the point where national leaders pay serious attention, and governments are supporting major efforts to mitigate those threats. Billions of people are at risk, among them your own family and friends. Yet you recall the dinosaur paradigm and realize that the impending collapse of civilization might save *Homo sapiens* from extinction at a later date. Suppose you are in a position of leadership. Do you support aggressive efforts to forestall catastrophe or do you favor letting it happen to save our species? One of these choices is disastrous beyond comprehension, but you have no way of knowing which one!

A great hero saves civilization leading us to false confidence and self-extinction.

A mad scientist kills 99% of humanity. This leaves a low-stress low-tech world population and saves our species from extinction.

Plausible Ironic Scenarios

My advice: avoid this grim choice altogether. Resign your position of leadership, and devote all your attention and resources to some means to ride it out. Save humanity by saving the younger fecund members of your own family, and other folks with whom you create a survival colony in some safe refuge.[117] The refuges discussed in Section 3.2 require foresight and public funds. Even if they are ready in time, which seems unlikely, they can accommodate only the lucky few. The rest of us will be left to fend for ourselves. Do-it-yourself survivalism may be your only fallback.

My advice is that we, the knowledgeable few, save humanity from extinction by saving ourselves. Forget about saving the world because we need all our limited time and resources to protect ourselves from as many hazards as possible. This is a selfish approach, which I am reluctant to condone; however, sharing limited resources with too many others might lead to failure.

3.4 Your own survival colony

If you set out to form a colony by polling your friends and neighbors, chances are you will find few if any takers. We need a worldwide register of potential colonists where each one can find others living in reasonable proximity. Accidental clusters can organize themselves into colonies with complementary skills. One such registry exists at the website of the Lifeboat Foundation.[118] Trouble is, people are not registering fast enough to organize colonies in a reasonable time. However, this may change suddenly when world events scare everybody.

Individual traditional preppers are often obsessive about one particular hazard.[119] Your colony must deliberate and make a calculated gamble. Since you cannot prepare for all possible hazards, you select the ones your pooled resources are best able to withstand. If you own some major asset, a ship for example, the obvious gamble is the one that uses that asset to best advantage. Otherwise, if the choice is not obvious, be a little reluctant to commit until you see some evidence of the most likely catastrophic threats developing.

Below are some possibilities.

Far south

Build a refuge (bug-out location in the jargon of preppers) where oceans meet in the far south. Since water has high specific heat, these oceans provide an enormous heat sink against global warming. The far south is also protection from nuclear war/winter since all nuclear weapons and their targets are located in the Northern Hemisphere. Possible locations include New Zealand's South Island, Tasmania, or Tierra del Fuego at the tip of South America. In any of these locations you should admit local people to your colony to insure friendly relations. In New Zealand they can include Maori, which would improve the colony's genetic diversity. In both Tasmania and Tierra del Fuego the indigenous people were largely exterminated. The Southern Alps of NZ offer refuge from rising sea level. The Central Highlands of Tasmania offer altitudes up to 1.6 km (5300 feet).

Tierra del Fuego

One possible refuge is the entire town of Grytviken, South Georgia Island. Your colony would have no trouble defending its larder from natives since there are none. (People work there providing services to tourists on their way to Antarctica.) Mountains are a refuge in the event of rising sea level.

Grytviken, South Georgia Island

Whatever location you choose, the expense will be great. A simple rehearsal in which your colony charters a jet to the refuge and lives there for a week or two will cost in excess of $100k. In a real emergency, you may need armed guards to protect your jet from hijackers. (Unless you are the hijacker!)

Filtered air

If contaminated air is approaching and you cannot escape, you can at least take refuge behind air filters. Perhaps all members of your colony live in one metropolitan area, and your refuge is a big centrally located structure sealed airtight for positive-pressure air filtration. NBC (nuclear, biological, chemical) filtration systems are commercially available, but they may not suffice. If you live near the Black Sea, you should certainly have the ability to remove hydrogen sulfide for reasons explained in Section 2.2.1. Wherever you live you should watch reports on changes in ocean circulation since you may need to prepare for Peter Ward's "green sky" scenario, a real possibility. If possible you should have a sophisticated laboratory for testing air, both for toxic chemicals and airborne microbes. You want the ability to make whatever type of filter is appropriate and to cleanse and refresh filters as needed. (major $$$)

You should have hazmat suits for those who venture outside. They exit and enter the refuge from an airlock at the exhaust end of the air path. In addition you have the usual survivalist stuff: living quarters, water supply, a deep larder, independent power generator and fuel, and means to repel intruders (Golden Horde) including firearms if necessary. (more $$$)

Seastead

This refuge is a ship or marine platform that stays far enough offshore to avoid whatever contagion or other badness is contaminating the land. Colonists are brought on board via boat or helicopter, perhaps residing first in a quarantine area before admission to the ship as a whole.

3.5 Save the wealthy

Neo-survivalists who have registered as survival colonists with the Lifeboat Foundation were asked if they could provide some major asset in an emergency that would define the character of their survival colony. It might be a habitat such as a ship or a building, or some means of transportation such as a private jet to carry people to a faraway refuge, or a helicopter to shuttle them to a local refuge on short notice. So far, only one candidate has anything to offer except ordinary tools and skills.

People who understand my analysis of survivability, Chapter 4 below, generally agree that it is reasonably valid, and many who don't understand look at my credentials and give me the benefit of the doubt. But none of them are moved to get actively involved **now**. Their lives are too busy; maybe later—mañana, that mythical time that never actually arrives. (As a tourist in Scotland, I was surprised to hear *mañana* used in that sense along with the saying, "Never do today what you can put off till tomorrow." One chap added, "Tomorrow? We Scots rarely feel that sense of urgency.") In summary, attempts to recruit ordinary people leave me with a sinking sensation.

However, there are exceptions, wealthy people whose ordinary needs are already fulfilled. Entrepreneurs are building luxurious survival habitats for them, and they are buying, even now before the first scary event has happened. Denver developer Larry Hall has acquired surplus Atlas missile silos in Kansas and is converting them to luxury condominiums.[120,121] You can purchase a half-floor unit for $1.5 million, or a full-floor unit for $3.0 million. Each silo has 8 residential floors and several more for common functions: lounge, exercise, health care, movie theater, pool and spa, hydroponic food, and much more. Hall's first silo is sold out, and he is now taking reservations in the second.

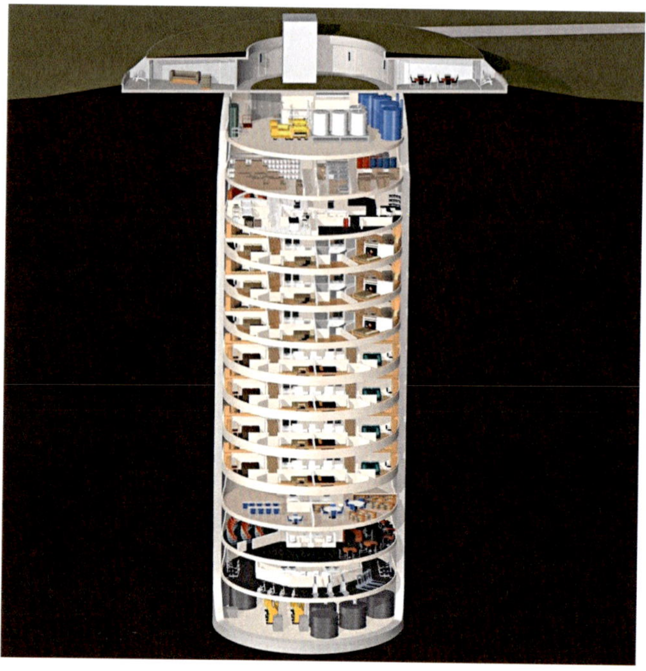

Survival habitat in a missile silo in Kansas[122]

Robert Vicino of Del Mar, CA has formed a company Vivos[123] that is selling space in an underground bunker in Indiana that accommodates 80 people. The cost is $50,000 per adult, $35,000 per child, which includes everything they need to survive underground for at least one year: food, clothing, shoes, recreation, and much more with the luxury of a 4-star hotel. The facility has NBC (nuclear, biological, chemical) air filtration and its own off-grid electric power generators. The company also makes Quantum underground shelters of any size, which they will install discreetly on your own property.

Vicino also purchased a huge artificial cavern near Atchison, Kansas that he planned to convert to a survival habitat. However, he canceled the plan for safety reasons, but of course he or someone else could reinstate this or some similar plan if and when conditions topside deteriorate to the point that the risks are worth taking. The cavern was originally dug as a limestone mine. After that operation ended, the U.S. Army bought it and used it as a storage facility. It has a concrete floor that Vicino planned to use as a huge parking lot where residents would live in their recreational vehicles.[124] It is 100 to 150 feet (30 to 45 meters) beneath the surface where the natural temperature is constant in the low 70s °F. The shelter would accommodate more than a thousand RVs and about 5,000 people in about 45 acres (18 hectares).

Yet another Atlas missile site in the Adirondack Mountains of northern New York is being converted to a luxurious survival habitat. Silohome[125] has a private airport. Log houses on the surface have secret passages to the Launch Control Center, which has two levels. The top level has a kitchen and commons, the bottom level two master bedrooms. The missile tube is not yet developed. The plan is to build up to ten apartments, one per floor.

Perhaps you find it distasteful that wealth should be the criterion that decides who survives. Other qualities such as health, intelligence, and dedication to worthy causes would be more satisfying criteria. Get over it! We do not have time and resources to be picky; just save whoever is most savable. Otherwise, the most advanced survivors may be rodents, or worse yet, cockroaches. After another 100 million years they would probably evolve into a second humanoid species, but that species cannot attain modern technology and industrial development. Secondary species will be stuck at the level of waterwheels and tools made from wood, leather, and stone. Progress beyond that depends on accidental discoveries of things that are no longer found on the Earth's surface: rich ores, native copper, petroleum oozing from the ground, and so forth; see *AW*, Section 5.8.

Nugget of native copper, about 4 centimeters, now rarely found outside of museums
Wikipedia commons, thanks to Jonathan Zander

Our galaxy may contain many secondary humanoid species that are stuck in just this manner. Perhaps we would be in contact with a technological species on one of these planets if its primary species had survived. However, this trap does not seem to fully explain Fermi's paradox.[126] (Where is everybody?) If one extraterrestrial humanoid species exists, it seems likely hundreds exist, and some of them would have suffered mild calamities that warn them in time to prevent extinction. So Fermi's question remains, "Where are they?"

Back on Earth, if you have an urge to save mankind, emulate Larry Hall and Robert Vicino; they have the right idea. In the process you take care of your own family as well. Hall has kept one of his silo condominiums for himself, and no doubt Vicino has made provisions. These two men do not have the full picture of survivability as presented in this treatise, in Bostrom's tome,9 and elsewhere, and so there is much more you can offer to wealthy neosurvivalists. For example, sell them things they can use for barter after the financial system collapses.

Build a survival habitat for your wealthy clients in the far south where cold southern oceans meet. Use local labor and make friends with locals; you will need friends when law and order break down. Include locals in your colony, especially young women; we need mothers for the next generation. Some of your colonists must comprise a militia ready and able to repel invaders.

Are you a pilot qualified to fly private jets? Offer your services to fly wealthy survivalists quickly to whatever refuges they may own in remote places. They will have to include you and your family in their colony so that you will have the incentive to do your job in extreme emergency when money may be worthless. Or are you a helicopter pilot? They may need transport for short distances if the streets are congested when the emergency hits. These suggestions are only a beginning. Possibilities for sales to wealthy survivalists go on and on, especially after a frightening event increases their numbers and their determination.

3.6 Sabotage?

Perhaps the most frequent widespread breakdown in our civilization is electric power outage.[127] The electric grid has an inherent instability: an unexpected interruption in one circuit does not instantly stop the huge spinning mechanical generator shaft, which then sends a surge through the other circuits it serves, thus endangering them. Engineers have devised safeguards, but some risk remains. The northeast blackout of 1965 affected more than 30 million people in Canada and US, some of them powerless for 13 hours. This was not the world's biggest outage, but the cause was known, human error in setting a protective relay.

Was the technician who made that error aware that he was the cause? If so did he feel remorse? In any case, there is a tiny chance that he saved civilization from destruction! We tend to build things that are dangerously complex and interconnected; recall hypercoherence, Section 2.7.9. We need reminders of the risks they entail. Of course the blackout of 1965 quickly faded into history except in the minds of some executives in power companies. But for a little while the general public, especially in the Northeast, was more aware of the dangers of size and complexity, and so a few decisions here and there were tilted in favor of simplicity. It is just possible that one of those decisions saved civilization or possibly saved humankind from extinction.

Ironically a small dose of bad things can be a good thing. (Recall the dinosaur paradigm.) Genetics gives us a classic example: a small number of Africans have a defective gene that gives them immunity to malaria. However, an unfortunate few get two copies of the defective allele, and they suffer from sickle-cell anemia. Their red blood cells are misshapen, and they have ailments that reduce their life expectancy. Thus genetic adaptation to malaria supports a small proportion of this mutation, but not a large proportion that would make sickle-cell prevalent.

Similar reasoning may apply to people with hacker mentality, those with a fiendish desire to outsmart others in ways that wreak havoc. Cooperation is a mainstay of our civilization, so why has evolution not completely eliminated hacker types from the population? Perhaps for the same reason it did not eliminate sickle-cell anemia. The tribe or nation that has a small proportion of these people is more robust than those who do not. Perhaps we need hackers to tweak the system and expose its weaknesses.

So, a question to normal readers who are *not* hacker types: suppose you see our civilization growing dangerously hypercoherent, too dependent on things that are too complex and fragile, and suppose you have a once-in-a-lifetime chance to commit an act of sabotage that makes your point, and you are reasonably sure you can get away with it. Contrary to your instincts, will you actually do it?

For example, we are becoming ever more dependent on the Internet. Cloud computing is a recent example. Instead of buying hardware and software to do a job in-house, people buy the capability as a service that companies provide via the Internet. More interconnected; more interdependent; more vulnerable. An event which causes the Internet to be inaccessible for a month would force us to recognize our dangerous overdependence, without devastating long-term consequences. Are you willing to bring down the entire Internet for about a month if you get the chance?

3.7 Resignation

Perhaps you expected this chapter, *How to save the human race*, to be more public-spirited by emphasizing things that society can do as a whole to improve everybody's survival prospects. Perhaps you expected a list of new laws and public policies to propose to your elected representatives with the idea that change may actually happen if enough readers write to them. Well, there was some of that in Sections 3.1 and 3.2, industry on the moon and refuges here on Earth. However, those of us who understand and accept the top-down analysis in Chapter 4 are a tiny minority, too few to influence legislation or attract funds either from governments or big philanthropy.

Moreover, you probably noticed an overarching tone of resignation to a degree of ignorance and corruption in government that we must expect to continue. Suspicions of corruption appeared earlier such as the U.S. Congress' failure to levy a tiny tax that would stop high-frequency trading in the stock market as discussed in Section 1.4. Resignation is apparent in the section above that seriously suggests sabotage, plus my willingness to abandon the public at large, team up with the wealthy, Section 3.5, and save only a small number, perhaps only one survival colony.

I am a citizen of the U.S. having no dealings with foreign governments beyond customs at their ports of entry. Although this limitation colors my advice; I suspect that other democracies have similar low levels of corruption and/or shortsightedness that limit what their neo-survivalists can hope to accomplish by government participation.

Let me conclude this chapter with yet other examples of government failure that support an attitude of resignation. The U.S. Congress refuses to raise the absurdly small excise tax on gasoline, 18.4¢/gallon. A greater tax is sorely needed both to reduce consumption of fossil fuel and to pay for repairs to infrastructure, especially roads and bridges.

Many nations have stopped minting coins that have no practical value. However, the U.S. still produces pennies at a cost of 2¢ each. In most cities pedestrians do not pause to pick them up off the sidewalk. The cause of this absurdity is campaign contributions from the zinc industry. (The copper coating is very thin.)

The financial crisis of 2007 revived an old expression, "too big to fail." Some financial institutions are so big that their failure would have disastrous consequences, and so the government had to bail them out at taxpayer expense. This is a terrifying concept; look at it from the viewpoint of a top manager at one of these institutions. He is considering a risky scheme that will make lots of money if future economic trends cooperate. If it works, he gets a big bonus. But if the economy sours, his scheme fails, but it is not his fault; he blames the economy. Then he negotiates a government bailout and gets a big bonus for skilled negotiation. So think about his incentive! If small companies were filling the role of this big one, each company knows it is small enough to fail, and hence avoids foolish risk. Only a cocky few would do something daring and either fail or win big, which is capitalism working at its best.

Alan Greenspan, longtime chairman of the U.S. Federal Reserve, said, "If they're too big to fail, they're too big." Accordingly he favors breaking them up.

Economist Willem Buiter has another idea,[128] levy a tax on bigness that pays for the costs of government regulation. Why not both?

The best way to serve the public interest with minimal regulation is to have a tax on bigness adjusted so that companies too big to fail will divide voluntarily to reduce their taxes. Ideally the feds should create a board similar to the Federal Reserve that maintains and tweaks a formula for computing bigness tax. The measure of size should include such factors as annual sales, annual profit, market value of stock, number of employees, number of shareholders, and domination of their market. A big company can destroy a small city if it closes a plant that is the city's major employer, and so the formula should also include some measure of payroll dominance in their locale.

In a few companies the economies of scale may be so important that they remain big and pay the tax. So be it. The revenue then pays the government's cost of regulating them.

Big companies have ways to cheat that small ones cannot afford. Big guys can put their corporate headquarters in overseas tax havens. They can lower their prices and undercut small competitors just long enough to bankrupt them, and then raise their prices again. There are laws about such practices, but it takes time and money to find infractions and prosecute them. And so on. A tax formula can be adjusted to target offenders one at a time and bring them in line. A federal bigness board can do this without going to court, proving guilt, and enriching droves of lawyers. While the tax also costs ethical companies, it costs their competitors as well, so the playing field remains level.

Companies often merge to achieve economies of scale. They can eliminate duplicate activities and departments; this is one aspect of hypercoherence discussed in Section 2.7.9. The motto is to be "lean and mean." Whoa! A modest amount of fat is a good thing; it can save your life during famine. Moreover, working in a small company is fun! When something bothers you, you can stroll into the president's office and discuss it. (If he is consistently too busy to talk, then find another job. Skilled managers make things run so smoothly that they seemingly have endless time to talk.)

A final reason for small size is to make more jobs. As computers and robots acquire more human skills, they take over ever more jobs until we can no longer afford economies of scale. Robots now do most of the storage and retrieval of merchandise in warehouses. Machines answer telephones, and so on. Not long ago law firms hired rooms full of young lawyers to plod through dusty old law books looking for judgments that would establish precedent in cases similar to their own. Now a search engine does this in one second or less. Word-processing software has greatly diminished the demand for typists and secretaries, and websites for planning travel and making reservations have also eliminated jobs for secretaries and travel agents. In the aftermath of this devastation, job duplication in small companies is one of the last few ways to create jobs for humans.

So, in conclusion, what is the probability that governments will make tax laws to keep companies small? Zero, of course. Hence my attitude of resignation bordering on cynicism.

Chapter 4. Numerical estimates of survivability

The hazards discussed in Chapters 1 & 2 involve many imponderables, so one cannot expect a numerical estimate to be very accurate. Nonetheless, we should do what we can. This is the main subject of my book, *Apocalypse When?*, in which Chapter 4 contains separate numerical estimates for the survivability of our civilization and for our species, *Homo sapiens*. In particular, I estimated the half-life of our civilization to be about a century, which is consistent with Martin Rees' hunch.1 Unfortunately, subsequent events show that the actual risk is much greater, and the true half-life of civilization falls in the range of 20 to 50 years.

What does it mean to quote a range of half-life? Ordinarily an unstable system (such as a radioactive atom) has exactly one half-life. As explained earlier, if we had survival statistics for hundreds of expired humanoid species on Earth-like planets throughout the galaxy, then we could indeed derive one value of half-life. But these data are not available, and so the true half-life is unknown, and we are stuck using probability theory to estimate its range. The result, 20 to 50 years, is clearly unacceptable and demands an intervention, most likely the AI Nanny.

4.1 Types of survivors

Let us distinguish two kinds of survivors. The first is things that wear out, decompose, or obsolesce at some characteristic age:

- individual animals die (humans, 90 yrs; mayflies, a few days)
- mechanical things wear out (car, 400 Mm = 250,000 miles)
- drugs expire (aspirin, 4 years)
- food rots (Cold milk spoils in a few weeks)

Let us call these *limited survivors*. Fig. 4 shows green timelines for individuals in a statistical sample. The second thing dies a bit prematurely, while the others live approximately the characteristic lifetime. The oldest (first) at time *now* is destined to have a short future, the youngest (last) the longest. In other words, *survival prospects dwindle with age.*

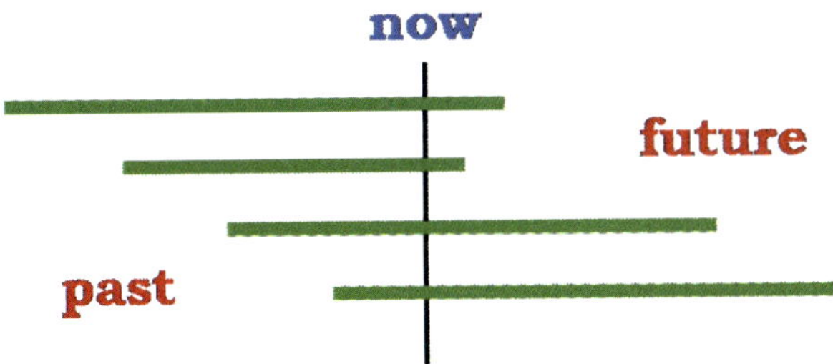

Fig. 4. *Limited survivors* having a characteristic age Their survival prospects dwindle with age.

The second kind of entity, *unlimited survivor*, has no characteristic age. Any specimen might last for days or centuries:

- business firms
- stage productions
- species, ours or
- civilization
- ethics (slavery, dueling, and such)
- nations
- space program
- zeitgeist
- political parties

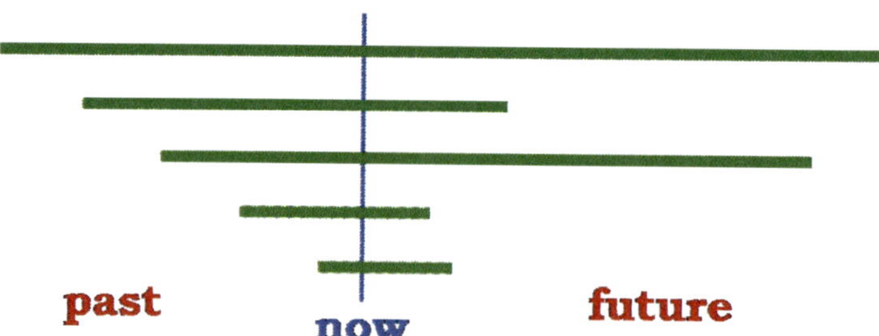

Fig. 5. *Unlimited survivors,* no characteristic age
Survival prospects increase with age.

Many folks are surprised to learn that survival prospects for *unlimited survivors* **improve** with age, Fig. 5. Their surprise is amazing, because the *expectation* that the oldest will have the longest futures already resides in our instincts, but we rarely articulate it at the conscious level. Consider a few examples: If a knick-knack store opens in your neighborhood and then goes out of business six months later, you are not surprised. If you return to the neighborhood of your childhood and find a business prospering that opened only a month before you moved away, you may be surprised that it has lasted so long, and even more surprised if it then fails six months later after having lasted all those years.

The age of something sets a time scale for the survival we expect in the future simply because past endurance attests to its robustness, while very young things may be frail or maladapted to their surroundings.

Philosophers Monton and Kierland[129] explain this very cleverly. You are visiting the Geyser Intergalactic Park and find a geyser spouting water. Beside it a digital stopwatch tells you that it has been spouting for 10 minutes. Then you find a second geyser nearby where the stopwatch tells you it has been spouting for 10 years. While you stand around a few minutes, one of them stops. Which one? Of course it's the first; you would be most amazed if the 10-year spout suddenly stopped.

Note that the group of timelines in Fig. 4 fills an area that looks vaguely like a parallelogram, while the group in Fig. 5 is vaguely triangular. This is simply a graphical representation of the same dichotomy: limited survivors' prospects dwindle with age; unlimited survivors prospects improve.

Individual humans are limited with a maximum age of about 90 years. However, our civilization, age about 100 centuries, is unlimited. It may endure another thousand centuries or it may expire in decades. Likewise, our species, which has lasted 2,000 centuries with modern anatomy, may last a million centuries or maybe less than one. Of course *unlimited survival* is an ideal that is never fully met, and indeed examples that follow show the longest lived entities, typically about 15%, dying off slightly faster than the ideal rates. If they did not, our world would be clogged with ancient things that have not expired fast enough to make way for new ones.

This treatise concerns only two entities, the human race and our civilization, not individual people, so from here on we discuss only *unlimited survivors.*

4.2 Two numerical approaches

There are two ways to attempt a numerical estimate of survival probability (survivability), bottom-up or top-down. Bottom-up analysis begins with a vast database about the present and recent past and then extrapolates it into the future by means of numerical simulation. One normally runs the simulation many times with different random events in each run. One can also change assumptions between groups of runs. Some results vary wildly with the changes, while others are more robust. Bottom-up has the advantage that one can do "what-if" experiments. For the case of human survival, one might ask, *What if* solar energy completely replaces fossil fuel? Perhaps the best known bottom-up analysis is the one by the Club of Rome estimating the limits to economic growth.[130] The Club has accepted a sequel, *Mankind at the Turning Point*, as its second official report.[131]

To do this for human survivability, we need a list of present and future hazards including dates when each hazard begins and ends and the probability per unit time that it causes a disaster of a specified magnitude. These so-called risk rates might be expressed as percent probability of happening per decade. The list would be long, the dates and risk rates highly speculative, and some future hazards would be overlooked. I do not know how to estimate risk rates for any of the hazards discussed in Chapters 1 & 2, nor have I found any such estimate in any of the books and papers on human survivability. Thus bottom-up is out of the question.

Top-down analysis uses some abstract principle that transcends the details in bottom-up. My top-down analysis in *AW* uses about 140 equations and this treatise only about 50 in the main text and another 50 in the appendixes. By contrast, the first Club of Rome model used about 1,000 equations, and the second 200,000.[132] So if you slog through the details of a survival model in order to assess its credibility, you might prefer my top-down approach.

Suppose we have a new design for a machine and want to know its feasibility. A bottom-up analysis would calculate the force on every gear and wheel, the pressure in every pipe, the tension in every pulley, and so on. One would learn lots of detail, which may be valuable, but the tedium makes errors and omissions likely. Again, independent review is difficult because the reviewer must slog through all the same details. By contrast, a top-down analysis would first check conservation of energy. The energy input must equal the energy output plus energy lost as heat (friction) plus any energy stored. A second check would verify that overall entropy increases. This is a measure of disorder. One can decrease entropy locally, but this must be offset elsewhere by an equal or greater entropy increase. And so on.

o—O—o

A recent paper gives top-down analysis of survivability. Motesharrei et al[133] made a mathematical model that explains collapse of societies in the manner of the Roman Empire, the Han, the Maya, and many others. Their analysis draws on mathematical models used by ecologists to study time variations in the number of predators and their prey. For example, the rate of change in the number of prey is their birth rate times the number of prey, minus the number of predators times their predation rate. And so on.

In this analogy human population replaces predators, and nature in general becomes the prey. However, human society is more complex, and so Motesharrei et al expand the model to four time-varying quantities: number of elite, number of commoners, wealth, and nature. Their equations have sustainable solutions, in other words feasible happy outcomes. But societies like ours are not inclined toward those outcomes; instead they doom themselves through overuse of resources exacerbated by economic stratification, the number of elite compared to commoners.

This paper aroused controversy: One headline screamed "According to a NASA-funded study, we're pretty much screwed."[134] Huffington Post UK picked up the story with "Civilisation is doomed warns Safa Motesharri's NASA-funded study;"[135] also The Guardian.[136] Although NASA did fund the study indirectly through the University of Maryland, the emphasis is misleading because NASA does not endorse the results. Otherwise, all three media reports treat the paper fairly.

Keith Kloor wrote a scathing critique of this study in *Discover* magazine's Collide-a-Scape,[137] which is merely vague posturing. Kloor supports his critique with reviews by three professors, one of whom is an anthropologist, another a philosopher. I suspect that these scholars are math-phobes who feel threatened when reminded that a measure of mathematical rigor can be applied to studies that once lay exclusively in their domains. A constructive review would delve into the author's equations and explain which one is in error, or show which assumption in the mathematical model does not reasonably approximate the real world, or possibly change the choice of variables. I fault *Discover* for publishing a dismissive critique that should have been constructive.

Here is my constructive review: Their model probably does not apply until the aftermath of a global catastrophe of the sort predicted here. Until then, the high probability of catastrophe overwhelms the quantities in their model. Moreover, I think they need a fifth variable, technology. They do discuss it, but argue that technology's effects balance out. However, it has more effects than the ones they discuss, for example medical care and contraception.

4.3 Gott's predictor

Let us begin our top-down analysis with the simplest case and then generalize it in steps until it has all the features we need to apply to human survivability. Let us define numerical survivability as the probability G that an entity survives for a future of at least F, in other words a formula that estimates G for any given value of F. In the jargon of mathematics we say that G is a function of F, which we often denote as $G(F)$. If we write G(7 yrs), that means the probability that the entity is still alive 7 years from now as estimated by putting $F = 7$ into the formula for G. For our case of human survival, consider the huge statistical sample of possible human futures. Then for any future time F, $G(F)$ is the fraction of those possible futures in which humankind is still alive at time F.

J. Richard Gott III, an astrophysicist at Princeton U., showed how to estimate the survivability of an entity when you know only its age, nothing more.[138] Figure 6 illustrates his formula. Each timeline represents the lifetime of the entity in question, which is divided into quarters Q1 through Q4. An observer encounters the entity at a random time, and somehow she determines its age *A*. In part a) of the figure, she happens to arrive exactly at the end of Q1, which means that the entity's future is exactly 3*A*. However, the probability of exact timing is infinitesimal, and we want to investigate finite probabilities, so let her arrive anytime in Q1. If she tarries until time 3A, she will find the entity still alive as shown in part b) of the figure. But if she arrives in any of the other 3 quarters, it will be dead after 3A.

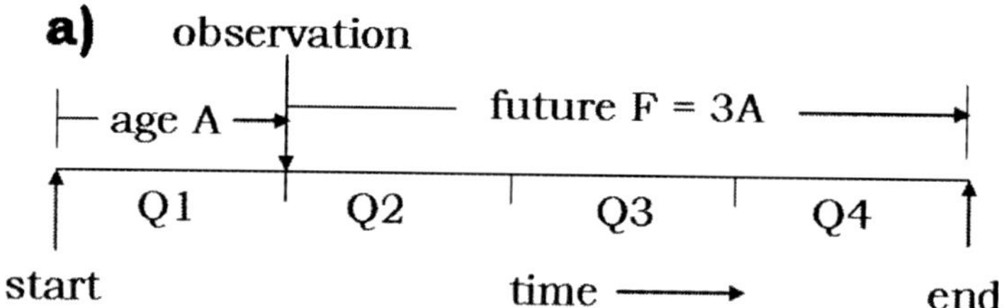

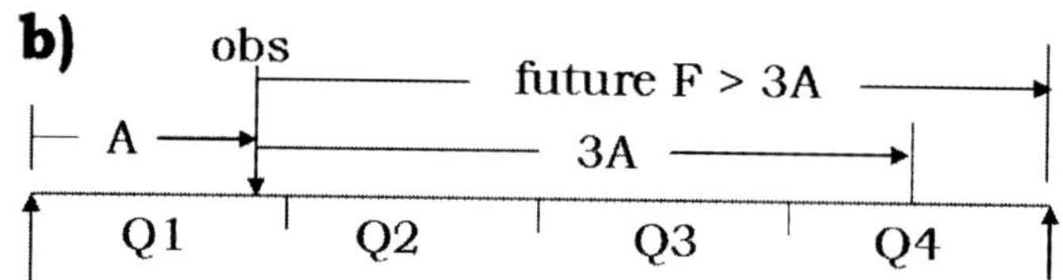

Thing is alive at future F=3A with probability ¼.

Fig. 6a & b. Timelines for Gott's survival predictor

If the observer's arrival time is not special in any way, it is reasonable to assume that arrival in Q1 occurs with probability 1/4, in which case $G(3A) = 1/4$. Thus we see that knowing the entity's age has predictive value, although additional information might show that her arrival time is somehow biased, in which case probability of arrival in Q1 may differ from 1/4. Knowledge of this difference may produce a much improved estimate of G.

Figure 6c shows another example in which an observer arrives in the last quarter of the thing's life again with probability 1/4. He tarries and sees the thing expire before time A/3 has elapsed. So it dies with probability 1/4, hence survives with the remaining probability 3/4. And so G(A/3) = 3/4.

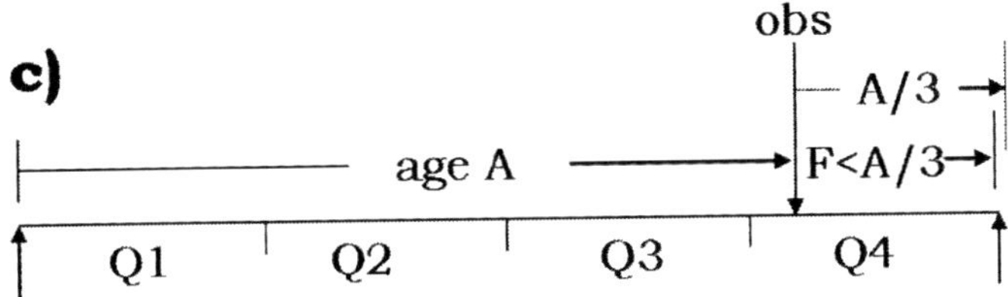

Fig. 6c. Timeline for Gott's survival predictor

Appendix B derives the general formula, namely

$$G(F|A) = \frac{A}{A+F} = \frac{1}{1+F/A} \tag{2}$$

where the notation $G(F|A)$ means the survivability G for future F when age A is known, or simply G as a function of F given A, the vertical line denoting *given*. You can easily verify Eq. (2) for the two examples above by showing that

$$G(3A|A) = 1/4, \text{ and } G(A/3|A) = 3/4.$$

For example, put $F = A/3$ in the first form of Eq. 2 and find

$$G\left(\frac{A}{3}\middle|A\right)=\frac{A}{A+A/3}=\frac{1}{1+1/3}=\frac{1}{4/3}=\frac{3}{4}$$

Think of F in Eq. 2 as a measure of future risk exposure, i.e. jeopardy, the greater the future in question, the more opportunities to expire. And think of A as a measure of proven robustness, risk exposure already survived. Then it seems natural that survivability should be a decreasing function of the ratio jeopardy/robustness, just what we have in the second form of Eq. 2.

Note that the median future, defined as $G = 1/2$, occurs when $F = A$ since Eq. 3 then gives $G = 1/(1+1)$. Curiously, the mean future is infinite, which is not obvious. In a statistical sample, the mean can be dominated by one or two specimens that live far longer than any other, whereas for the median the same exceptional specimen has no more effect than an ordinary specimen.

Figure 7 is a graph of Eq. 2 that shows the three examples mentioned above at $G = 3/4$, $1/2$, and $1/4$.

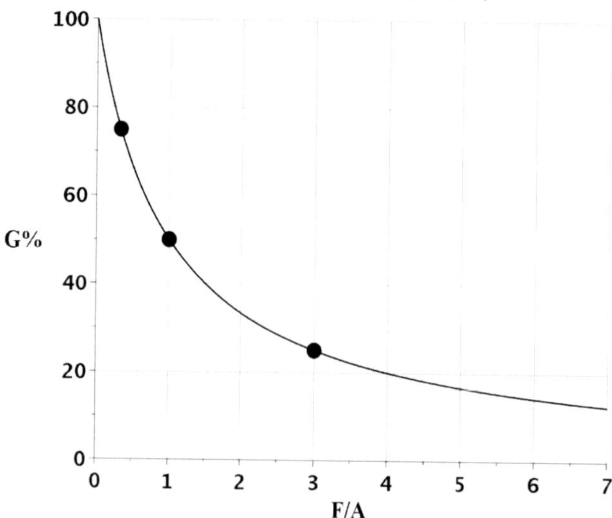

Fig. 7. Gott's predictor showing points discussed in the text

o—O—o

The idea that one can assign equal probabilities 1/4 to arrival in each of the four quarters is an example of the "principle of indifference" so named by economist John Maynard Keynes.[139] It was formerly known from the early 18th century as "the principle of insufficient reason": if an event has n mutually exclusive outcomes, and you have no grounds whatsoever for thinking any one more likely than the others, then you may assume each has probability $1/n$.

This principle is both useful and full of pitfalls as many scholars have explained. For example the late Martin Gardner in his column in *Scientific American* asked us to consider four playing cards, two black and two red, shuffled and dealt facedown.[140] If you pick two, what is the probability they are the same color? One person reasons, "There are 3 equally possible cases, both black, both red, or one of each, so the answer is 2/3."

"Wrong," says another. "There are 4 cases: both red, both black, card x is red and y is black, and vice versa. So the answer is 2/4 = 1/2."

In fact, both are mistaken. The first card you draw has a color. Of the 3 remaining cards, one has the same color, the other two are different. So the probability of the same color on the second draw is only 1/3. More formally, the number of combinations of 4 things taken 2 at a time is

$$\binom{4}{2} = \frac{4!}{2! \times (4-2)!} = 6$$

of which we count two as successes, red-red & blue-blue, so the probability is 2/6 = 1/3.

All this means is that the principle of insufficient reason must be applied with caution taking great care to look for sufficient reasons why one outcome may be more likely than another.

When Gott first published his predictor in 1993 it was met with much skepticism. Some say the principle of insufficient reason is unjustified. Others object on various philosophical grounds. I choose not to review these arguments here because they are simply not germane. I have tested Gott's predictor against published survival statistics as described below. It clearly works well, and that is all that matters for the subject of this treatise. I encourage readers who want tidy logic and philosophy to pursue the published arguments, but they require a different mindset that would be distracting here. Readers so disposed can find a good review and commentary in a paper by Morton and Kierland.[141] Their footnotes contain references. A related concept is Brandon Carter's Doomsday Argument championed by John Leslie.[142] Other commentators include Bostrom,[143] Buch,[144] and Goodman.[145]

In his original paper Gott stressed that his formula applies only if the time of observation is an ordinary time, not birth, nor a time of great duress, nor a transitional time that radically changes the entity's risk exposure. Then Gott broke his own rule by applying his formula to human survival, during 1993, a time of radical technological change when humans for the first time ever are developing means of self-extinction. Thus Gott's estimate of survival time was wildly optimistic. This is the issue his critics should have raised, but they did not. My main effort in *AW* was to generalize Gott's predictor in such a way that it does work in this time of rapid change.

Gott substantiated his formula by publishing a list of survival data on 44 Broadway stage productions[146] plus numerous comments on other survival dates ranging from the Berlin Wall to the Tories control of the House of Commons. His analysis of these data was superficial; nonetheless, it served as a strong hint that his formula could be developed into a practical tool for forecasting simply by comparing survival data that was already available in published literature. None of the other cited scholars took this hint; some "refuted" his approach without even looking at readily available data to see whether they might be mistaken. (In one curious paper,[147] philosopher Elliott Sober confessed in his Note 5 that an anonymous reviewer demonstrated the validity of Gott's theater statistics, and yet the journal published Sober's refutal anyhow. Go figure!) In the end, my readers and I may be the only people using Gott's formula as a practical forecasting tool!

4.4 Accuracy

Gott's predictor gives a best estimate of survival probability based on age only, which means profound ignorance of many other details that influence the entity's survival. But these details exist nonetheless, and they do influence survival, and so we have no *a priori* reason to expect that Gott's predictor will fit empirical survival data very well, even though it is a best estimate given what we know. So I looked for published survival data for entities that would serve as proxies for humanity and give some indication of accuracy. The best proxies would be humanoid species on Earth-like planets throughout our galaxy, but apparently their survival statistics are not available. So I chose survival statistics for business firms and stage productions because they too consist of people striving for their entity's survival. Further discussion of this selection appears in *AW* on p. 3.

Plenty of survival statistics are readily available. I used about two dozen statistical samples to substantiate Gott's predictor as shown in *AW* Figs. 8–16. Results were favorable except for one serious discrepancy, stage productions that opened in London during 1900–01, which appears in *AW* Fig. 14, p.48. Attrition was normal for 83 productions, after which the remaining 42% died off too rapidly. By 1904 attrition was completely normal again with only 4 shows dying off faster than Gott's theoretical rate. Those last few presumably suffered some obsolescence like the *limited survivors* discussed in Section 4.1.

Only one discrepancy out of a couple of dozen! We appear to be extraordinarily lucky, but of course something more than luck is working to our advantage. It has something to do with human intuition. For example, I began my analysis of the London theatre using the number of performances of each stage production rather than its time duration even though Gott's original predictor is explicitly about time. I did this with scarcely a thought because it is obvious that performances, not time, tended to exhaust the potential supply of paid admissions to the theater. Thus the formulas based on Fig. 6 still apply by changing the label on its axis from time to cumulative number of performances.

As another example, suppose we calculate the survivability of a clay pigeon in a shooting gallery, its hazard exposure is the number of shots fired at it rather than the passage of time, because the clay pigeon is in jeopardy only during times of the day and days of the week when people are firing at it. Hence, for this example F and A in Eq. 2 refer not to time but to numbers of shots.

Our apparent luck is evidently something in the workings of the human mind. We are not skilled at estimating absolute probabilities of events. However, our intuitions do sense what variable is most relevant and how to adjust the formulation to make it work.

o—O—o

Sometimes we like to inquire how long a thing will survive with a given level of confidence G. So let us invert Eq. 2 (solve for F) and find

$$F(G) = (1/G - 1)\,A \qquad (3)$$

Imagine that we are living in the early 20th century, perhaps 1920, and Gott's formula has already been invented. It seems like an ordinary time and so the formula ought to apply to human survivability. Let us use Eq. 3 to find humanity's survival time at G = 90% confidence. The result is

$$F(0.9) = A/9$$

For our species and our civilization this gives

human species:	A = 2,000 centuries;	F = 220 cnt
civilization:	A = 110 centuries;	F = 12 cnt

These results are utterly unreasonable; at the pace man-made hazards are proliferating and interacting, our civilization is unlikely to last 1 century, much less 12, as explained below in Section 4.9. But this example does not invalidate the formula because it is not typical. Like the London theater in 1900–01, it is an outlier carefully selected to illustrate the limitation. In 1920 mass self-destruction was not possible, and nobody could have known that 50 years later technology would be on a roll producing myriad possibilities. Now that we know this, we ignore the 1920 prediction and start again somehow taking this new knowledge into account.

4.5 Initial survivability (life expectancy at birth)

Let $Q(T)$ denote the probability that a newborn entity survives for at least lifetime T. This is just an important special case of G where age is zero, namely life expectancy at birth:

$$Q(T) = G(T\,|\,0) \qquad (4)$$

However, Professor Gott stressed that his original predictor is valid only when the observer's arrival is not special in any way. Thus it is no surprise that his formula fails at age zero since the outset of a new entity (birth) is its most special time until it expires: Equation 2 would give $G(T\,|\,0) = 0\,/\,T$.

We can modify Eq. 2 so that it does apply at age zero. Consider a stream of interested observers visiting the entity and arriving at a constant rate R, and you are a random member of that stream. In the discussion of Fig. 6, the observer arrives at a random time. Now, instead of time, let us interpret the horizontal lines in Fig. 6 as a scale that represents your position in the stream. When you arrive, those ahead of you are past observers numbering $R{\times}A$ while those behind you are future observers numbering $R{\times}F$. Substitute these quantities for A and F in Eq. 2, the R factors cancel, and the equation remains the same—so far.

The need to modify Gott's predictor at or near age zero arises with entities whose birth is a noteworthy event, things like businesses that have a grand opening and stage productions that have a dress rehearsal and an opening night. During that event, a cluster of N additional observers appears. Depending on the business, these may include investors, critics, founder's family, and so on. So add N to the group ahead of you, let J denote N/R, and Eq. 2 becomes

$$G(F \mid A) = \frac{N + R \times A}{N + R \times A + R \times F} = \frac{N/R + A}{N/R + A + F} = \frac{J + A}{J + A + F} \qquad (5)$$

Since A enhances survivability and J adds to A, one can think of J as representing midwives that help the entity survive birth. Now you come along as an ordinary observer, and your arrival is not so special anymore having come after at least N others.

This argument based on a stream of observers is used again below to derive another important generalization of Gott's predictor, which is then confirmed by another method. Thus the observer stream appears to be a powerful approach. The offset that changes A in Eq. 2 to $A + J$ in Eq. 5 resembles a similar offset in a related probability problem, Laplace's rule of succession described briefly in Appendix A.

Using Eq. 5, Eq. 4 becomes

$$Q(T) = G(T \mid 0) = \frac{J}{J + T} \qquad (6)$$

Appendix C substantiates this formula using another approach.

Sanity check: The fraction of newborn entities that will survive for time $A + F$ is $Q(A+F)$. Let us calculate that same fraction one step at a time. The probability of surviving to age A is $Q(A)$, and the fraction of that fraction that continues to survive the second interval from A to $A+F$ is $G(F|A)$. Hence, the fraction surviving both intervals is the product. Equate the two expressions

$$Q(A+F) = Q(A)\times G(F|A) \tag{7}$$

and solve for G using Eq. 5 for Q:

$$G(F|A) = \frac{Q(A+F)}{Q(A)} = \frac{J}{J+A+F} \times \frac{J+A}{J} = \frac{J+A}{J+A+F}$$

which agrees with Eq. 5.

Equation 6 is the form used in *AW* to compare with published survival statistics. (A nonzero value of A would exclude specimens that do not survive to that age and might seem contrived to bias the data.) Starting on p. 41 in *AW*, Sections 2.2 and 2.3 provide many plots of Q from published data in Figs. 8 through 16. All the values of J in these figures were derived from the survival statistics by regression analysis for lack of any insider information about preparations for the opening events. If we assume these J values are valid, the agreement is quite good as discussed in the preceding section. One example appears in Fig. 8 below where the points are real statistics and the solid curves are plots of Eq. 6.

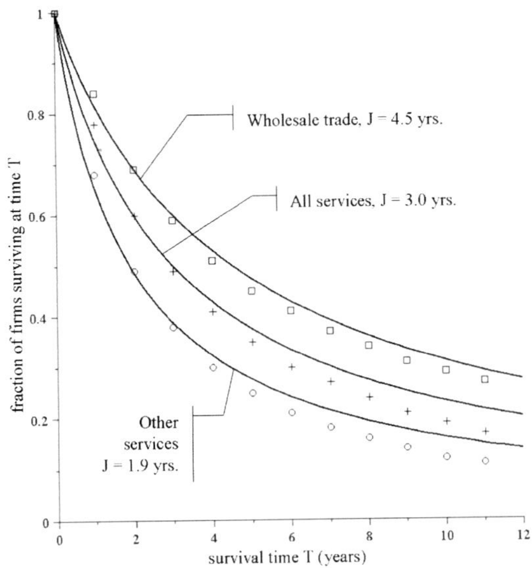

Fig. 8. Longevity of service firms in Canada[148]

o—O—o

Published survivability data do not always appear as graphs like this. Often they are simply lists of individual entities along with survival times *T*, perhaps businesses that opened in Kalamazoo from 1950 to 1960. So how do you convert such a list to points that you can plot on a graph and compare to *Q(T)* as in Fig. 7? First, enter the data in a spreadsheet. One of the columns gives *T*, the survival time for those that have expired, which are the majority because the median time for survival is only about 4 or 5 years. Assign the surviving firms some arbitrary long duration, say 999 years, which serves as a placeholder. Sort the rows using the *T* column in descending order, which puts the surviving ones on top, the longest lived expired firms next, and so on to the shortest lived on the bottom. Next, create a new column called *rank* and assign rank = 1 to the entity in the top row, rank = 2 to the next, and so forth to rank = *N* for the last, N being the number of specimens in all. For a particular entity of rank R and duration T, R equals the number that were still alive at age T, while the statistically expected number is $N \times Q(T)$. Equate the two:

$$R = N \times Q(T) \quad \text{or} \quad Q(T) = R/N \tag{8}$$

which is the desired result that you list in a final column. When you plot Q versus T, leave out the surviving entities at the top of the spreadsheet. They have served their purpose by adjusting the rank of the longest-lived expired entity.

This concept of rank invites a comparison to Zipf's law,[149] which appears in *AW* pages 52 & 53. American linguist George Kingsley Zipf studied the frequency of words in natural languages and found that their frequencies were approximately inversely proportional to their rank. In English *the* is most frequent at 6.4%; *of* is next with 3.0%, about half, and *of* is third with 2.6%, about a third of 6.4. Rank 10 is *his* with 0.75, about a tenth the frequency of *the* with rank = 1.

4.6 Accelerating hazard exposure

In this section we modify Gott's predictor so that it applies in our modern world with its accelerating hazard rate.

Suppose that we have some sort of meter that keeps a running tally of risk exposure in the manner of gas and electric meters for houses. Let us denote this tally by Z. Sometimes we use the notation $Z(t)$ where t in parentheses is a reminder that Z is an increasing *function* of time t, and if we write $Z(2014)$ it means the cumulative hazard exposure from the earliest man-made hazards to the year 2014. To estimate future survival, we shall need some theory that projects $Z(t)$ into the future. This theory appears in the next section.

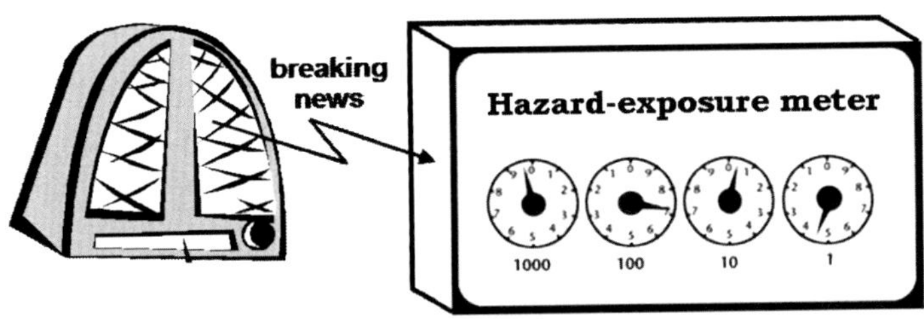

In the discussion following Fig. 5 and again in the second paragraph following Eq. 2 we noted that an entity's past survival indicates its robustness. This becomes quantitative when expressed as the hazard exposure accumulated over the entire past:

$$\text{robustness:} \quad Z_p = Z(\text{now}) - Z(\text{at outset}) \tag{9}$$

Similarly, when we inquire about the entity's future prospects, we must estimate values of its hazard exposure at time F in the future, namely $Z(\text{now} + F)$, which gives us a quantitative estimate of its future jeopardy:

$$\text{jeopardy:} \quad Z_f(F) = Z(\text{now} + F) - Z(\text{now}) \tag{10}$$

Since Z_p enhances survivability while Z_f threatens it, one might expect that survivability is a decreasing function of the ratio Z_f/Z_p. And we should not be surprised when it turns out to be the same function of a ratio that we already have in Eq. 2, as we shall see in Eq. 11 below.

Let us postulate a stream of observers just as we did leading to Eq. 5. Imagine that a race of exohumanoids has been watching Earth out of curiosity for the past two billion years. At first they stopped by every 78 million Earth years to check what geology was doing and whether the cyanobacteria (blue-green algae) had modified their swim stroke. But now with high-tech humans racing toward the Singularity, their curiosity has peaked and they swing by every 167 days.

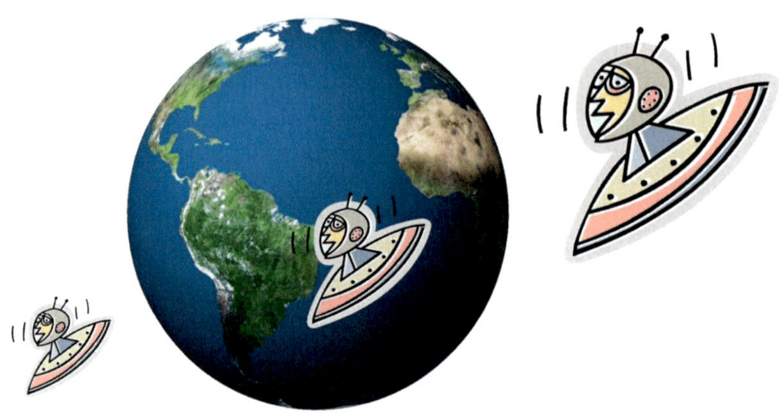

Whenever the word spreads that something interesting is likely to happen, knowledgeable observers come around to watch. Interesting times tend to be hazardous. (Recall the ancient curse: "May you live in interesting times.") People doing research in human survival (myself, for example) are probably doing it now only because we live in a century when our survival is threatened. Had we lived in the 19th century, chances are our thoughts would never have turned to this line of inquiry.

Newcomers to the stream of Earth observers will tend to fill a gap where the increment in Z is rather big since that gives them the best chance of seeing events that others miss. Thus observers tend to space themselves in the stream at equal increments of Z. Let z denote that increment. Then the observer arriving now is number Z_p/z in the stream, and those behind him at future time F number Z_f/z. Just as we did leading to Eq. 4, let us now interpret the horizontal timelines in

Fig. 6 for Gott's predictor as a scale that represents the observer's position in the stream. Thus the before and after counts in the stream replace the quantities A and F in Eq. 2, and we find

$$\text{survivability:} \quad G(F) = \frac{1}{1 + Z_f(F)/Z_p} \qquad (11)$$

which is the decreasing function of Z_f/Z_p anticipated beneath Eq. 10. (The notation *(F)* in the denominator reminds us that Z_f is a function of F through Eq. 10.) As time passes, exposure Z_f grows at an accelerating pace and survivability wanes. The median future occurs when $Z_f = Z_p$.

Prof. Gott's original formulation carried the restriction that the observer arrives at an ordinary time, which suggests that risk rate λ should be assumed constant. Thus $Z_p = \lambda \times A$ and $Z_f = \lambda \times F$ and $Z_p/Z_p = F/A$. Making this substitution in Eq. 11 restores Eq. 2, Gott's original predictor. Thus Eq. 11 is the simplest and most obvious generalization of Eq. 2.

This argument based on a stream of observers is questionable on grounds that it presumes to second-guess their motives and schedule. A different approach in Appendix D strengthens the argument. This is how it goes in this treatise: nothing is perfectly rigorous, but yet each approach fills a weakness in the others until the whole becomes reasonably convincing.

4.7 Estimating hazard exposure

In principle one could hire a panel of judges to follow world news, and keep a tally of cumulative hazard exposure. Every time something dangerous happens, each judge increments the tally by an amount from 1 to 10 based on her assessment of the risk. Their tally Z jumps in sizable increments at random times when something scary happens, for example a new measurement of the melting of arctic ice due to global warming.

This scheme is not amenable to future projections because we cannot predict future hazardous events. We need to find a smooth approximation to $Z(t)$ by assuming that it is proportional to some measure of human activity that creates the serious hazards. For example, the total number of published papers in natural sciences and engineering is a measure of progress in high technology, hence a reasonable proxy for high-tech threats such as artificial microbes, robotics, genetic engineering, and the like. Similarly, gross world product (sum of the gross domestic products of all countries) measures low-tech activity, which makes it an appropriate proxy for threats such as greenhouse gases, pollution, and rapid transportation, which would aggravate a pandemic by spreading the contagion too fast for quarantine. World-wide power consumption, Fig. 9, is another good measure that encompasses both high- and low-tech.

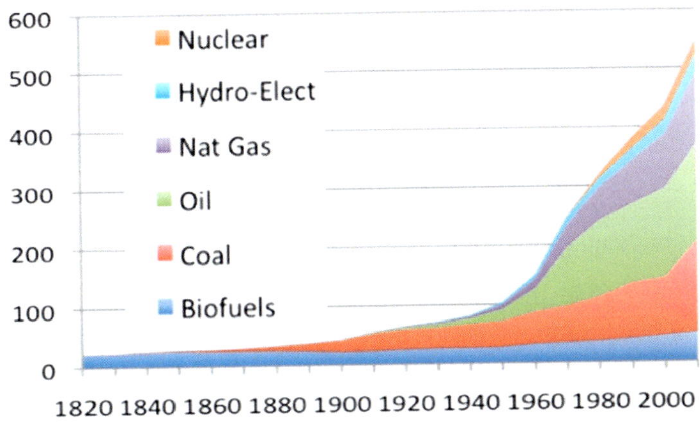

Fig. 9. World power consumption, exojoules per year[150]

One of the better single measures is electric power consumption, Fig. 10, because it emphasizes high tech somewhat more than low, and indeed high tech is more hazardous than low. We need not choose just one measure of *Z* but rely instead on a composite of various measures of hazardous progress.

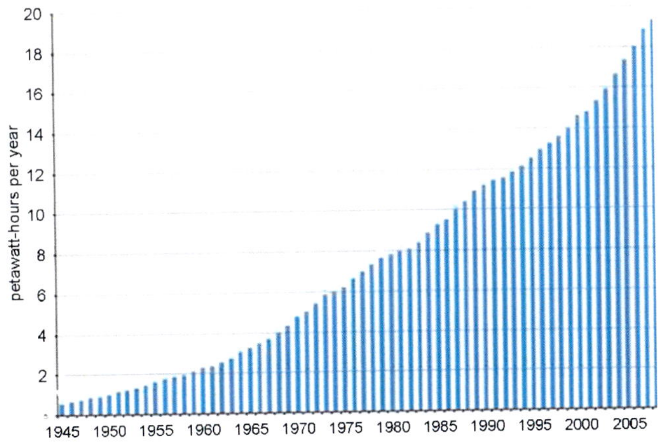

Fig. 10. Worldwide consumption of electric power[151]
Original source: International Energy Agency databases

Whatever proxy we use for hazard exposure, we cannot estimate future survival unless we have some means to make future projections of hazard exposure that will be reasonably valid for a couple of centuries, barring global catastrophe or other drastic change. A simplistic projection that merely extends graphs like Fig. 10 with straight lines would not suffice: we need a mathematical model.

To formulate this model, assume that the annual increment in hazard exposure, risk rate ΔZ, is proportional to the population p of people creating the risk of self-extinction. This assumption is obvious for those risks like climate change that are caused by everybody's bad habits. It is also reasonable for the risk of extinction by a single mad scientist because the probability of his birth and warped worldview is proportional to p. So whom do we count in this population? Everybody? Or only those deemed most dangerous?

Opinions differ. Folks who worry about disease should count people in the most crowded germ-breeding areas of Africa and Asia. Those who fear robotics and artificial intelligence run amok should count both the high-tech nations that make them and the world's myriad sweatshops that make it affordable. Those concerned about deforestation should count everybody: lumber companies provide machinery, transportation, and money; affluent people everywhere create the demand; and homesteaders in the forests are all too willing to sell their timber rights and work as lumberjacks. In time they would raze the forests and jungles anyway for agriculture. Those who believe that consumption of resources is a big threat should count all affluent people plus many third-world nations that sell off their natural resources at an unsustainable pace. All of these judgment calls are too subjective, so let us count everybody. Just let p denote total world population.

Besides population, ΔZ is also proportional to some measure U of hazardous industrial / technical / scientific development that gives fanatics the tools and power to commit extinction. Hence,

$$\Delta Z = p \times U \tag{12}$$

Next we need an equation for U. No doubt there are differences between the set of hazards that threatens civilization, and the set that threatens the human race, but the distinction is not apparent from our top-down viewpoint, and so let us use the same U with the same equation for both entities. Differences between survivability of civilization and human race will appear later by way of another parameter.

The annual increment ΔU is again proportional to p, the number of people participating. There is also positive feedback since yesterday's technology enables today's and today's enables tomorrow's. And so ΔU is proportional to U raised to some positive power call it μ. Hence

$$\Delta U = C \times p \times U^{\mu} \tag{13}$$

where C is an undetermined constant. We never worry about undetermined constants because they appear in both Zs in Eq. 11 where they cancel in the ratio. Eq. 13 is Eq. 11 in *AW*. Some folks claim that quantities like Z and U are growing exponentially, which implies $\mu = 1$. In fact they do grow rapidly, but not *that* rapidly as explained beneath Eq. 11 in *AW* and substantiated by published statistics like Figs. 9 & 10 as we shall see later.

Equations 12 & 13 lead to differential equations that are easily solved, Appendix K in *AW*. The results are most readily expressed in terms of population-time *X(t)*, or pop-time for short, which is the sum of world populations for each year from the dawn of humanity to time *t*. Each year every person alive adds one more person-year to this pop-time tally:

$$X(t) = \sum_{\text{Adam}}^{\text{year } t} p(\text{each year}) \tag{14}$$

(This also equals the sum of the lifetimes of everyone who ever lived and died plus the current ages of everyone alive now. In other words, you get the same answer adding life-years one year at a time or one person at a time, the former being more practical.)

The solution for *U* appears in *AW* Eq. 12, namely

$$U = (X - X_o)^{\omega}, \quad \text{where} \quad \omega = \frac{1}{1 - \mu} \tag{15}$$

and X_o is the pop-time when humankind first became a threat to themselves. The equation for *Z* appears in *AW* on p. 81,[152] also p.194, namely

$$Z = (X - X_0)^{(\omega + 1)} \tag{16}$$

We need values for the undetermined constants X_o, ω, and μ in Eqs. 13, 15, & 16. I estimated these by fitting *U* to the general shape of hazard proxies such as those in Figs. 9 & 10 plus others in *AW*, namely Figs. 19 through 22 (in which the abscissas look like dates but are in fact population-time *X*).

Fig. 11 shows the finalists. I omitted patents because changes in law and judgments in cases of patent infringement affect their popularity. I omitted numbers of papers in *Nature* magazine because it has spawned other journals. Zinc and bromine are random choices for production of minerals. Rare earths represent applications in high tech. The earlier rare-earth points are 5-year averages; otherwise, the curve would be far more jagged. The upper electricity curve is for power plants worldwide, which presumably does not include vehicular generators nor sales of dry-cell batteries. The lower electricity curve is for US only, which shows later data having a bit of downturn at the end.

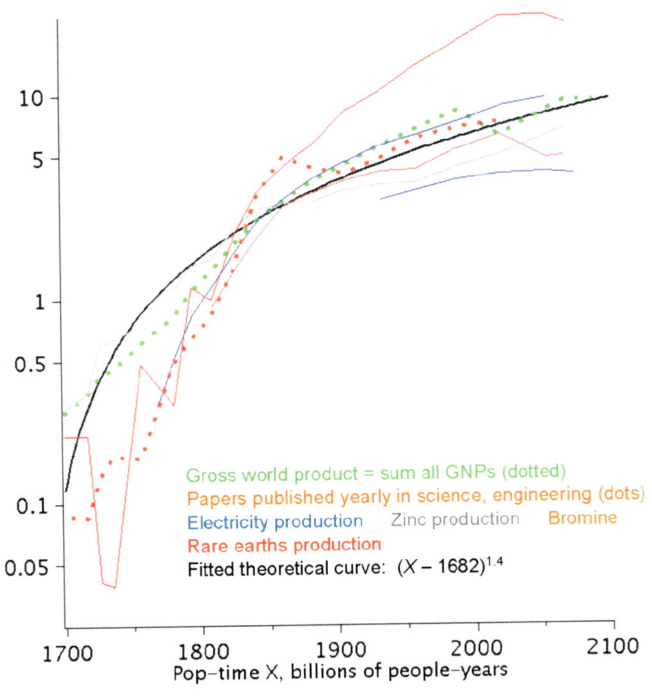

Fig. 11. Proxies for hazardous development, *U*

Vertical position of these curves has no significance because the scale is logarithmic and so vertical displacement represents a scale factor. These factors cancel in the ratio in Eq. 11. Results of the fit to the theoretical curve are

$$\omega = 1.4, \text{ hence } \mu = 0.286$$
$$X_o = 1{,}682 \text{ BPY in the year 1900 A.D.} \tag{17}$$

o—O—o

The quantities in Figure 11 are not suitable proxies for the extraordinary hazards of digital technology, which includes high-tech attacks like Stuxnet and the long-term possibility of unfriendly artificial intelligence. These threats require separate formulas like Eqs. 11 & 12, but let us use Y instead of Z as the symbol for cumulative exposure:

$$G_{dig} = \frac{1}{1 + Y_f(F)/Y_p}; \quad \Delta Y = p \times U \tag{18}$$

To evaluate the new U, we again need proxies for hazardous development, and Moore's law,[153] Fig. 12, is the most obvious one. The original version of this law applied to the density of transistors on a planar chip. Thus the exponential increase is doomed to fail when the size of each transistor reaches that of a single molecule. However, other measures of computer performance can take over and continue the exponential trend. For example, chips are still planar; stacking transistors in the third dimension is limited by the severe cooling problem. But eventually a solution will be found, and the trend will continue. Quantum computing[154] is another possibility that may extend an equivalent Moore's law beyond the molecular limit.

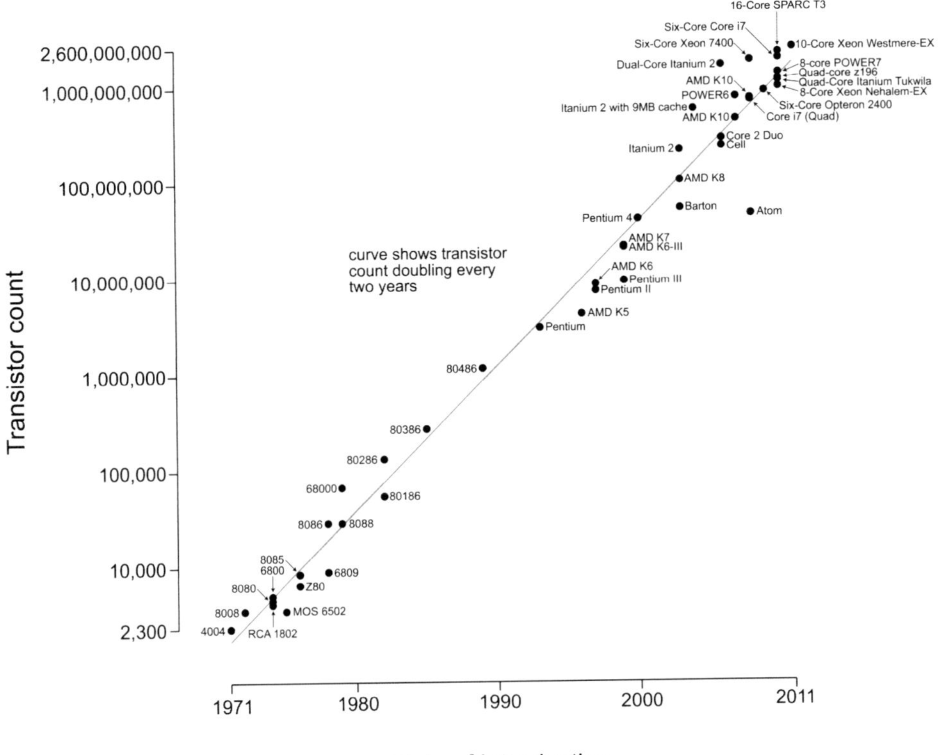

Fig. 12. Microprocessor transistor counts & Moore's law
from Wikimedia Commons

Figure 13 shows another version of Moore's law by Ray Kurzweil, which includes historical means of data processing.

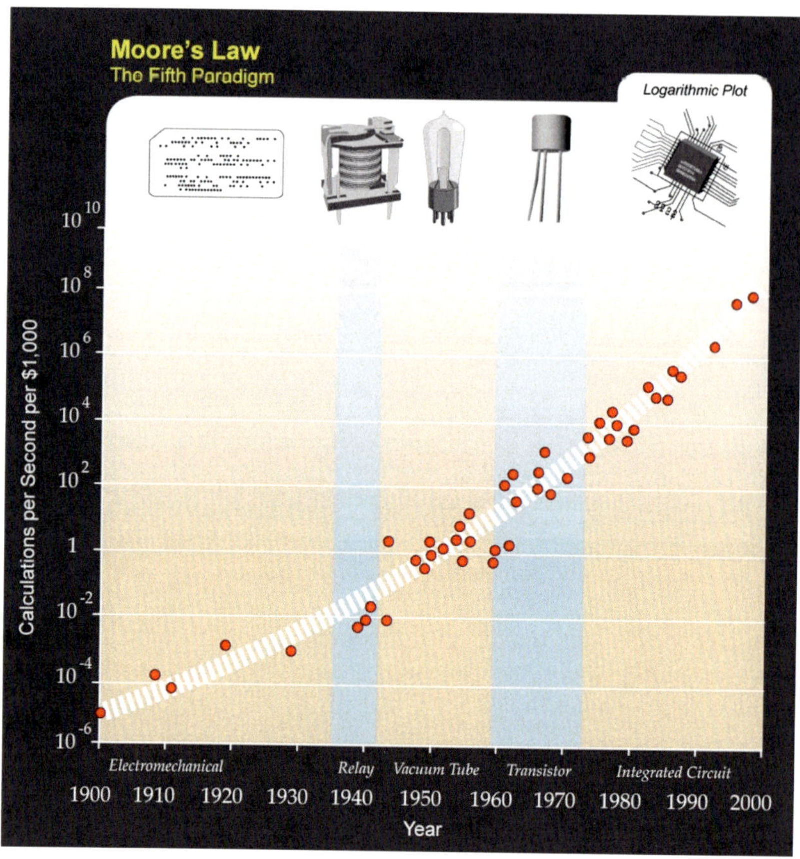

Fig. 13. Kurzweil's version of Moore's law
Courtesy of Ray Kurzweil via Wikimedia Commons

A graph of proxies that corresponds to Fig. 11 appears in Fig. 14. Note that the ordinate's covers 15 orders of magnitude in contrast to Fig. 11 with only three! The steep rate in increase is typically described as exponential in time, but it is not quite exponential when converted to pop-time as shown here. This allows us to reuse the power-law form for U in Eq. 15, except that Y is the symbol for the new group of hazards:

$$Y = (X - X_0)^{(\omega + 1)} \tag{19}$$

where the parameters that replace Eq. 17 are

$\omega = 24$, $\mu = 0.96$ (Exponential would be $\mu = 1.0$)

$$X_0 = 1{,}532 \text{ BPY in year } 1800 \quad (20)$$

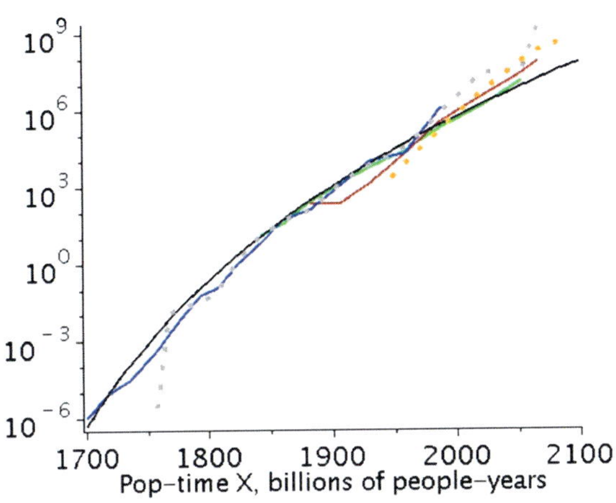

Fig. 14. Proxies for haz-dev in digital tech & AI

green — original Moore's law

blue — Moore's law modified, extended by Kurzweil

brown — typical hard disk capacity[155]

grey dots — best performance of supercomputer in FLOPS (floating point operations per second)[156]

orange dots — best 500 supercomputers[157]

black — best fit theoretical curve for projection

4.8 Triple jeopardy

As a simplistic summary of basic probability theory, *AND* means *multiply*, while *OR* means *add*. Examples: If you toss a coin *and* roll a die, the probability of getting tails *and* six is 1/2 × 1/6 = 1/12. Roll one die and the probability of 5 *or* 6 is 1/6 + 1/6 = 1/3. Survival involves a series of ANDs because the entity in question must survive Hazard 1 AND Hazard 2 AND ....

Actually the product (multiplication) rule holds only if the events are statistically independent; in other words, the outcome of one does not influence the probability of the other. Most hazards that we deal with are statistically independent. For example, the chance that an asteroid exterminates humanity is unrelated to the chance that a mad scientist does it. There are exceptions. For example, we'd like to have one factor for natural hazards and a second for man-made. However, the chance that nature kills humanity with a new contagion is related to the chance that mankind provides the rapid transit systems that defeats quarantine efforts. On the other hand, it is also related to the chance that man develops a vaccine in time. In the first exception the two effects reinforce; in the second they oppose. We have no reason to think that positive correlation is more or less likely than negative. Hence, in accord with statistical indifference, let us assume that hazards are statistically independent on average, so let us forge ahead and apply the product rule.

We can expand these ideas and factor our predictor into a product of probabilities of many independent risks or categories of risk. In principle there could be a separate factor for each hazard:

$$\begin{aligned} G &= G_1^{\alpha} \times G_2^{\beta} \times \cdots \times G_{24}^{\omega} \\ &= \left(\frac{1}{1 + F_1 / P_1} \right)^{\alpha} \times \left(\frac{1}{1 + F_2 / P_2} \right)^{\beta} \times \cdots \times \left(\frac{1}{1 + F_{24} / P_{24}} \right)^{\omega} \end{aligned} \tag{21}$$

where the exponents all sum to 1.0 ($\alpha + \beta + \gamma + \ldots \omega = 1$) and the pasts P include any applicable Js (for midwives) as in Eq. 5. (Eq. 21 is Eq. 8 in *AW*.)

In practice, the limited accuracy of input data would seldom justify more than two or three such factors. Any more would be counterproductive because we cannot establish the many parameters (exponents and Js) accurately enough to realize full theoretical precision. So let us re-aggregate factors in Eq. 21 into groups that represent similar hazards, have similar pasts, and depend on the same independent variable. This mental exercise of disaggregation and regrouping provides some insight: *exponents represent the number of different ways disaster can happen, i.e. statistical weight, while the ratios F/P represents risk due to inexperience.*

For human survivability we need exactly three factors. The following equation applies to survival of civilization; some changes in notation will extend it to the extinction case in Section 4.10:

$$G_{civ}(\mathit{future}\,|\,\mathit{past}) = G_m \times G_d \times G_n$$
$$= \left(\frac{1}{1+Z_f/Z_p}\right)^q \times \left(\frac{1}{1+Y_f/Y_p}\right)^v \times \left(\frac{1}{1+F/A}\right)^{1-q-v} \qquad (22)$$

The factors are ...

- G_m for ordinary man-made hazards, which has the form in Eq. 11 and depends on Z as in Eq. 16.
- G_d for digital tech (think Moore's law), which has risk exposure Y. This factor is an extreme case: its statistical weight is very small because it represents a highly specialized attack, but it has big impact despite its puny exponent because $F/P \rightarrow Y_f/Y_p$ grows rapidly, the 15 ormags seen in Fig. 14.
- G_n for natural hazards has constant risk rate and thus depends only on time as in Gott's original predictor, Eq. 2.

At one extreme, no natural hazards, $q + v = 1.0$; at the other extreme, no man-made hazards, $q + v = 0$. Civilization is vulnerable to both, so $q + v$ will be sort of middling, not far from 0.5.

o—O—o

The evolution of Eq. 22 from Gott's original predictor, Eq. 2, is justified here only by intuitive arguments. Equation 2 is a univariate function of time, while the new G is a trivariate in time and two measures of risk exposure, Z and Y. Can the generalization possibly be invalid? It is worrisome because intuitive theoretical arguments have piled up to an extent that empirical confirmation would be reassuring.

So what could go wrong? The expressions in parentheses seem valid in view of the interpretation of the ratio jeopardy/robustness that follows Eqs. 2 & 10. Surely the product rule applies. What could conceivably go wrong is that the sum of exponents in Eq. 22 might no longer be constrained to 1.0. I have not found a way to investigate this from basic principles. Probability theory can be mysterious like this. For example, despite logic problems Bayesian theory has gone from disrepute to wide acceptance.[158] And Zipf's law[149] inexplicably applies to myriad unrelated things from sizes of corporations to distribution of income.

During my research for *AW*, I digressed on a successful effort to substantiate the factored forms like Eq. 22 using statistics of stage productions. This was a bivariate case, the two variables being number of performances and lapsed time, both of which stress a production in different ways. Results confirmed the expected sum of exponents. Details appear in *AW*, Section 3.3 &

Appendix H. A brief summary appears in Appendix E below.

I am not aware of any multivariate survival formula like Eq. 22 in existing literature nor have any of my readers or lecture audiences suggested that one may exist. Perhaps this is an original contribution to probability theory.

o—O—o

Let us now limit our survival formula, Eq. 22, to the few centuries of interest in which $F << A$ as discussed in Section 2.1. For civilization's survivability, F/A may be as much as 5%, 5 centuries/100 centuries, but there is no way we can achieve accuracy of 5% in this analysis, so we can set the third factor = 1.0 regardless of its stat-wt. This agrees with Chapter 2, section 2.1 where we already noted that natural hazards are negligible over the time in question. The result is

$$G_{civ} = \left(\frac{Z_p}{Z_p + Z_f} \right)^q \times \left(\frac{Y_p}{Y_p + Y_f} \right)^v \tag{23}$$

We have now lost sight of the exponent $1 - q - v$, but it is still the statistical weight for natural hazards, and so $q + v$ must be small enough to leave reasonable stat-wt for nature. Compared to Eq. 22, the form of the expressions inside the parentheses is changed to prepare for the next step.

Let the time called "now" in Eqs. 9 & 10 be the year 2015, the reference date for this treatise. Population quantities appear in *AW*, Table 6, p. 75, but these require updating from 2009 to 2015 with the result

$$\begin{gathered} p = 7.3 \text{ billion;} \\ X(2015) = 2{,}088 \text{ billion people-years} \end{gathered} \tag{24}$$

Then substituting X_O = 1,682 and ω = 1.4 from Eq. 17 into Eq. 16 gives the result

$$Z_p = 406^{2.4} \qquad \& \qquad Z_p + Z_f = (406 + X_f)^{2.4}$$

and the first factor in Eq. 23 becomes

$$\left(\frac{Z_p}{Z_p + Z_f}\right)^q = \left(\frac{406^{2.4}}{(406 + X_f)^{2.4}}\right)^q = \left(\frac{1}{1 + X_f / 406}\right)^{2.4q}$$

Future pop-time X_f will be the independent variable in formulas and graphs that follow, so let us change the symbol to lower-case x, which is universally the most common symbol in that role. Making the corresponding changes on the second factor in Eq. 23 using Eqs. 19 & 20 gives our final predictor of civilization's survival:

$$G_{civ} = \left(\frac{1}{1 + x/406}\right)^{2.4q} \times \left(\frac{1}{1 + x/526}\right)^{25v} \qquad (25)$$

x = future pop-time

All we need now to evaluate G_{civ} are the exponents q & υ. The best way to find them is to do a regression analysis on a statistical sample of humanoid species on Earth-like planets in our galaxy. Alas, lack of data just leaves us guessing. *This is a huge problem, our biggest loss of accuracy.*

Regarding accuracy, I do *not* mean accuracy of predicting how long civilization will survive, but rather the accuracy of survivability curves such as those in Fig. 8. With a good q & υ we should get accuracies like 5, 10, 20% as *AW* demonstrated using survival data for business firms and stage shows. But left guessing, accuracies are more likely a factor of 2, or maybe 3. However, even this accuracy is much better than hunches that are not based on analysis.

Mathematically, the optimum recourse for unknown q & v is to use an average of Eq. 25 over all possible values of both q & v. This must be a weighted average that assigns great statistical weight (st-wt for short) to the most probable combinations of q & v, and the least weight to the least probable combinations as explained in Appendix F. If we use angle brackets to denote this average, Eq. 25 becomes

$$G_{civ} = \left\langle \left(\frac{1}{1+x/406} \right)^{2.4q} \times \left(\frac{1}{1+x/556} \right)^{25v} \right\rangle_{q,v}$$

which is the equation displayed on the front cover of this book.

Mathematically, st-wt is expressed as a probability density function (pdf). The most familiar pdf is the so-called bell curve, but that is not the appropriate choice to use here. Our pdf is a function of both q & v. It must be very simple and devoid of parameters; otherwise, it is or appears to be contrived to produce a result its author wants to see. The pdf we need for civilization's survival is developed in Sec. 4.9, which follows.

4.9 Survivability of civilization

Whereas extinction is well defined, the collapse of civilization is a fuzzy concept. Suppose a few cities in extreme locations (altitude, climate, latitude) survive the cataclysm, does it then qualify as a collapse? For our purposes the best definition of civilization is an infrastructure so advanced that human self-extinction is feasible. Thus the collapse of civilization ends the threat of extinction during some long aftermath.

Recall the survivability formula for civilization:

$$G_{civ} = \left(\frac{1}{1+x/406}\right)^{2.4q} \times \left(\frac{1}{1+x/526}\right)^{25v} \qquad (25)$$

where x = future pop-time

This applies if q & v are known, but they are not, so we need to formulate a pdf for these st-wts. It can be non-zero only for permissible combinations of q & v shown below in Fig. 15 as an area on the q,v plane. One restriction is that $q > v$ because q is the stat-wt of ordinary hazards whereas v applies to a limited class of high-tech hazards, and so the pdf vanishes on the tan-colored line $q = v$ in the figure. Below this line values of v become gradually more probable, so let us put a linearly increasing factor in our pdf to represent this:

$$\begin{cases} (q-v), & q > v \\ 0, & otherwise \end{cases}$$

Recall that the st-wt of natural hazards is $1 - q - v$. To prevent the sum $q + v$ from intruding on this, let us include a factor in our pdf that goes to zero along the line $q + v = 1$ shown in green in Fig. 15. A linear zero like the one above would not suffice because it would allow values of $q + v$ fairly close to 1.0. (Recall that natural hazards have strong st-wt even though their time scale is very slow.) So let us use a quadratic factor:

$$\begin{cases} (1-q-v)^2 & if > 0 \\ 0, & otherwise \end{cases}$$

Finally, the blue boundary at the bottom of the figure indicates $v > 0$, but v can be extremely close to zero because it represents digital tech, which has been on a wild ride (Moore's law) that ineluctably must end in a few decades. So let us include a factor that makes the pdf singular (infinite) at $v = 0$ but a weak singularity so that we can make the area under the pdf = 1.0, which simply means that the probability of something happening is 100%. The natural (not contrived) choice is the factor ...

$$\begin{cases} \frac{1}{\sqrt{v}}, & if\ v > 0 \\ 0, & otherwise \end{cases}$$

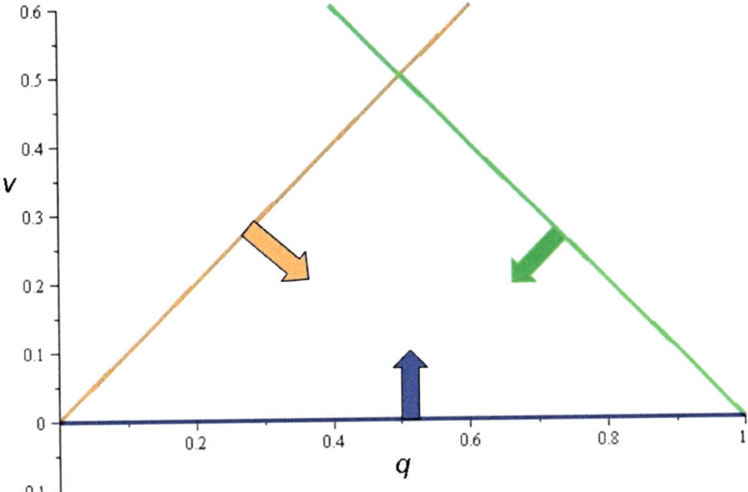

Fig. 15. Permissible area in the q,v plane

Multiplying these three factors synthesizes a plausible pdf, namely

$$W_{civ} = \begin{cases} \frac{20.88}{\sqrt{v}} \times (1-q-v)^2 \times (q-v), & \text{inside the triangle} \\ 0, & \text{outside} \end{cases} \tag{26}$$

which appears in Fig. 16 as a contour plot. The multiplier 20.88 is the so-called normalization. It makes the volume under the contour surface = 1.0.

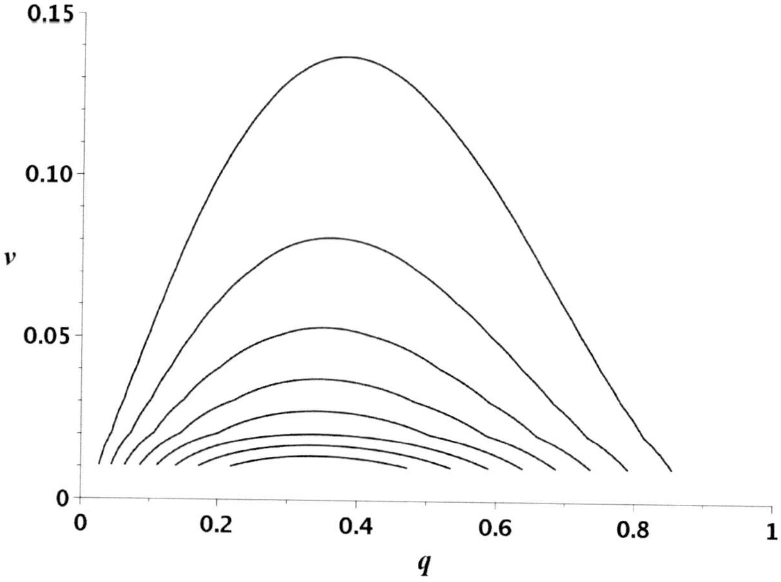

Fig. 16. Contour plot of the pdf for civilization's survivability

Let

$$n = 1 - q - v \tag{27}$$

denote the st-wt of natural hazards. Although n is not explicit in Eqs. 23 & 25, we should still look at it as a sanity check on our formulation. Appendix G shows how to calculate mean values of the three st-wts, which total 1.0. The results are

$$\langle q \rangle = 0.409,\ \ \langle v \rangle = 0.0455,\ \ \langle n \rangle = 0.545 \tag{28}$$

where angle brackets again denote averages.

The ratio $\langle q \rangle / \langle v \rangle = 9.00$. This is reassuring because the hazards of digital tech (v) are highly specialized, and so the ratio should be big. (Recall that q and v do not represent the full magnitude of their respective risks, but only the number of different ways they can happen.)

o—O—o

Appendix H derives civilization's risk rate from Eq. 25. In particular, Eq. H-5 gives the initial risk rate, which applies for the next few decades:

$$\langle R(x=0)\rangle = (4.3\langle q\rangle + 33\langle v\rangle)\,\%/\text{year} \qquad \text{(H-5)}$$

The mean values in Eq. 28 give the initial risk, namely

ordinary hazards — 1.8 %/year,
digital technology — 1.5 %/year,

total — 3.3 %/year.

Thus risk from digital technology is almost equal to risk from ordinary hazards.

One can easily compute the mean values of survivability, Eq. 25, using the method shown in Appendix G, and likewise calculate the variance and standard deviation from the mean. However, I am wary of these quantities because extreme outliers tend to distort them. For example, suppose a town has 20,000 residents of average wealth $50k, $1 billion in all. Suppose a man worth $9 billion moves there to be with his aging parents. The average wealth jumps from $50k to $500k, a factor of ten, but the median hardly budges, perhaps $20k to $21k. The latter is the more appropriate indicator of change because the character of the town has hardly changed from the addition of one billionaire.

Accordingly, let us express statistics of civilization's survivability as a median computed from Eq. 25 using our pdf, Eq. 26. The result is the dashed red curve in Fig. 17. The black curves on either side each represent probability 1/3 (meaning 1/6 on either side), so that the interval between them represents 2/3 probability.

Appendix I explains the mathematics for aggregating probabilities to obtain these curves.

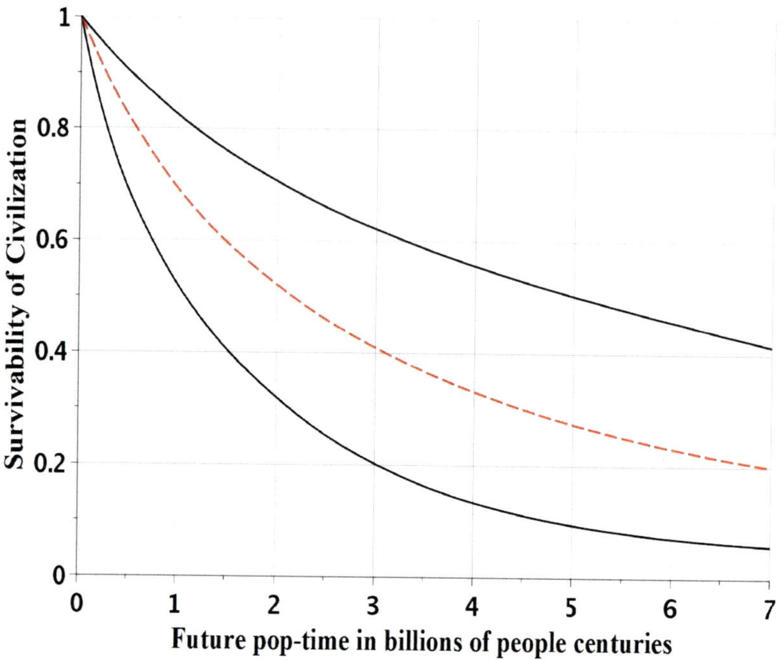

Fig. 17. Probability of civilization's survival as a function of future population-time in billions of people-centuries

A summary number to remember is the half-life of civilization, which appears in the figure along the 0.5 survivability level. The points where it crosses the black curves show that half-life falls between 1.1 and 5.1 BPC with 2/3 confidence. Or switching from centuries to years, the half-life range is 110 to 510 billion people-years with the median at 220. In the first edition of this treatise, the median was 200, only a 10% change, which indicates that the conclusion is fairly robust.

If world population goes from 8.0 to 9.0 billion during that future, then average population over the period from now to then will go from about 7.7 to 8.2 billion; let us say about 8 billion. This puts civilization's half-life in the range of 14 to 64 years, a frightfully short future! Children living now are likely to see the end of civilization. This is why we need powerful intervention as soon as possible. Supervisory artificial intelligence may be the only viable possibility. At this point you should be so worried that you drop everything else and devote your life full-time to survival issues!

4.10 Survivability of the human race

To find an equation for the survivability of our race, let us review Eq. 22 for civilization and note similarities and differences.

$$\begin{aligned} G_{civ}(\textit{future} \mid \textit{past}) &= G_m \times G_d \times G_n \\ &= \left(\frac{1}{1+Z_f/Z_p}\right)^q \times \left(\frac{1}{1+Y_f/Y_p}\right)^v \times \left(\frac{1}{1+F/A}\right)^{1-q-v} \end{aligned} \tag{22}$$

The factor for natural hazards, the far right here, is even more negligible for extinction because F is still five centuries or less, but now A is 2,000 centuries for our race instead on only 100 for civilization.

The same two categories of man-made threats apply represented by the ratios of *Z*s and *Y*s, but their st-wts (exponents) are much smaller for extinction because there are so few ways that the whole human race can be extinguished compared to the number of ways civilization can collapse. Extinction, the ultimate calamity, must reach the mountains of Tibet, the jungles of Amazonia, underground malls and subways of great cities, the Falkland Islands, and the remotest islets in the

South Pacific and Indian Oceans. It must be pervasive in the extreme, leaving so few survivors that they cannot find each other and assemble a tribe that would comprise a viable breeding stock, about 80 to 100 people.

Thus we need new symbols for stat-wts given in the following table:

Table of symbols for statistical weight

Entity at risk	Ordinary hazards	Digital technology
Civilization	q	v
Human race	r	u

(Underlined letters suggest mnemonics.) The following inequalities hold:

$$r < q; \;\; u < v; \;\; v < q; \;\; u < r \qquad (29)$$

As discussed above, the first two say that many of the hazards that threaten civilization are insufficient to cause extinction. The last two say that the st-wt of digital technology is small because the threats are highly specialized. There are relatively few ways that digital tech can harm us even though those few are quite dangerous.

The new stat-wt for natural hazards is $1 - r - u$, which is greater than $1 - q - v$ for civilization as a result of Inequations 29. Moreover, this acknowledges the great power that nature has demonstrated in prior mass extinctions—five being the number often named and described.[159] These were more thorough (so far) than the single man-made extinction, the one now in progress. However, humans were not present during the first five, so this could indicate a trend.

Our species survival is a more complicated subject than civilization's survival because extinction is not independent of civilization's collapse. Quite the contrary, civilization's collapse most likely destroys the man-made hazards that threaten extinction. Here we discuss only the setup and the results. Details appear in Appendix J.

Appendix H derives an expression for civilization's risk rate, Eq. H-4. To convert it to the extinction risk rate, simply change the symbols as indicated in the table above: $q \to r$, $v \to u$. The result is

$$R = p \times \left(\frac{2.4\,r}{406 + x} + \frac{25\,u}{556 + x} \right) \tag{30}$$

Recall that the denominators have units of billions of people years, so when p is billions of people, R is a fractional risk per year.

Consider a big statistical sample of humanoid races on Earth-like planets. To get a mortality rate for these species, we do not apply the risk rate to the whole sample, but only to the fraction that have *not* suffered a collapse of civilization, the others having been immunized by their experience for the few centuries of interest here. Hence, the mortality rate is the product of R in Eq. 30 by G_{civ} in Eq. 25:

$$\begin{aligned} \textit{mortality rate} = R \times G_{civ} &= p \times \left(\frac{2.4r}{406 + x} + \frac{25u}{556 + x} \right) \\ &\times \left(\frac{1}{1 + x/406} \right)^{2.4q} \times \left(\frac{1}{1 + x/556} \right)^{25v} \end{aligned} \tag{31}$$

You may think that the analysis of civilization's survival in Section 4.9 puts an immoderate emphasis on probability density functions. I did that to show that they are not biased to produce preconceived results. Well, now it only gets worse because Eq. 31 contains all four st-wts, two for civilization and two more for extinction, which makes our probability density function (pdf) a four-dimensional object. Still it seems necessary to derive this object from a basic principle because again the alternative would appear contrived. So from here on work is computationally intense since it involves integral calculus in five variables: r, u, q, v, & x.

We synthesize a pdf W_{hum} in a manner similar to Figure 15 and Eq. 26. It is the product of factors F_1 through F_5 that are nonzero only where essential inequalities are satisfied including the four listed beneath the table of stat-wts, Inequation 29. The first factor is

$$F_1 = \begin{cases} 1-q-v, & \text{if positive} \\ 0, & \text{otherwise} \end{cases}$$

This quantity is the stat-wt of natural hazards, which must be positive, in fact we raise F_1 to the sixth power, which seems contrived, but this is the power that gives the best agreement with Eq. 26, our previous pdf for q & v; see Fig. 18 below. Next,

$$F_2 = \begin{cases} q-v, & \text{if positive} \\ 0, & \text{otherwise} \end{cases} \qquad F_3 = \begin{cases} r-u, & \text{if positive} \\ 0, & \text{otherwise} \end{cases}$$

These factors express the fact that $q > v$ & $r > u$ since there are many more ordinary hazards than exotic digital ones, recall Inequations 29. Next,

$$F_4 = \begin{cases} q-r, & \text{if positive} \\ 0, & \text{otherwise} \end{cases} \qquad F_5 = \begin{cases} \dfrac{1}{\sqrt{u \times v}}, & \text{if } v > u > 0 \\ 0, & \text{otherwise} \end{cases}$$

These factors express the fact that $q > r$ & $v > u$ since civilization is more vulnerable than the human race. Moreover, the singularity (infinity) at $u,v = 0$ indicates that these statistical weights are very small just as v is very small for civilization's survivability.

Altogether now,

$$W_{hum} = 1.25 \times 10^5 \times F_1^6 \times F_2 \times F_3 \times F_4 \times F_5 \quad (32)$$

where the constant multiplier normalizes the hyper-volume of the 5-dimensional space to 1.0. Computing the five mean values of stat-wts using Eq. 32 and comparing to Eq. 28 for civilization's collapse yields ...

Ext: $\langle r \rangle = 0.212, \quad \langle u \rangle = 0.0135,$

$\langle q \rangle = 0.411, \quad \langle v \rangle = 0.051, \quad \langle n \rangle = 0.774$ (33)

Civ: $\langle q \rangle = 0.409, \quad \langle v \rangle = 0.0455, \quad \langle n \rangle = 0.545$

Agreement between the two values of ⟨q⟩ and ⟨v⟩ is quite adequate. Recall that nature's st-wt, n, is not expected to be the same in the two cases. For civilization it is 1 – q – v; for extinction it is 1 – r – u. As expected, natural hazards play a much bigger role in extinction because nature has often demonstrated her power to extinguish species. Appendix J gives further details. Eq. J-2 shows the pdf, Eq. 32, reduced to a single line.

Fig. 18 shows approximate agreement with W_{civ} in the q,v plane, which is the reason for the seemingly arbitrary sixth power of F1 in Eq. 32. Appendix J gives further details. Eq. J-2 shows the pdf, Eq. 32, reduced to a single line.

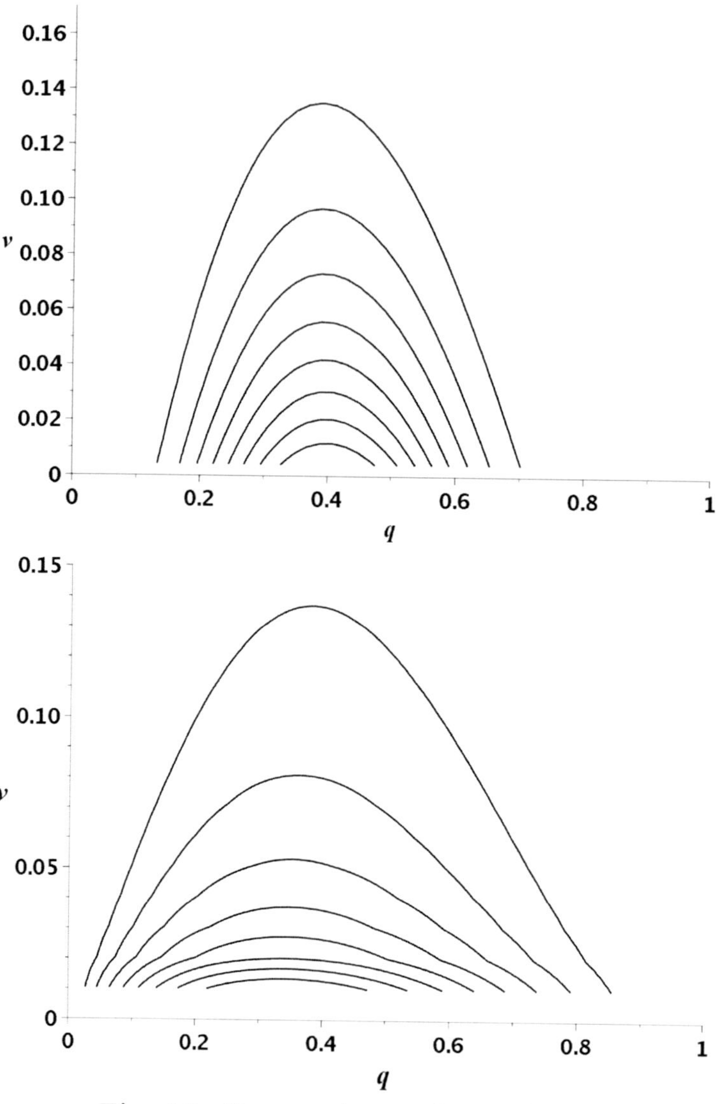

Fig. 18. Comparison of q,v planes

top: projection of W_{hum} in q,v,r,u space on the q,v plane
bottom: original, Fig. 16.

o—O—o

The next main task is to apply the mortality rate in Eq. 31 using the pdf described above, and to obtain graphs of the probability of extinction. Details appear in

Appendix J, final results in Fig. 19 below, the probability of human extinction as a function of future population-time. As in Fig. 17, the dashed red curve represents the median, whereas each black curve denotes probability 1/3 deviation from the median.

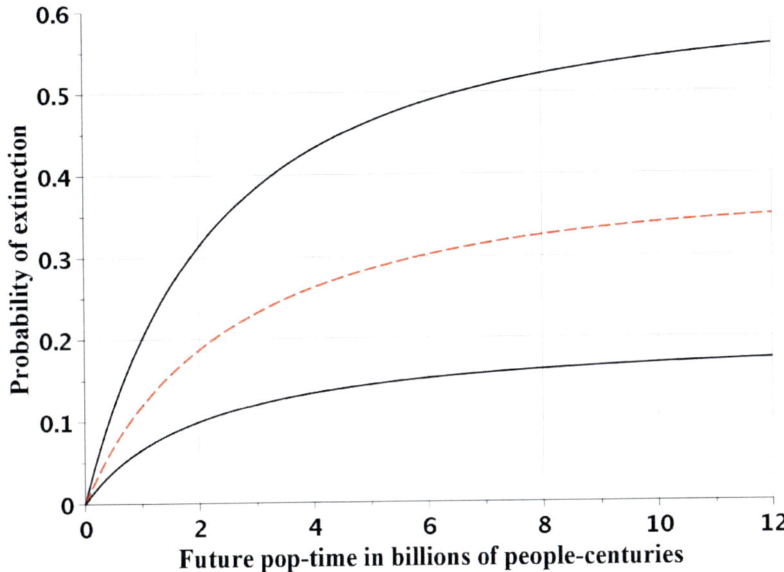

Fig. 19. Probability of human extinction as a function of future population-time in billions of people-centuries

A summary number to remember is this: After a century or two, our odds of survival are about 2:1; in other words probability of extinction is just about 1/3, survival 2/3. Let us review the exact meaning of these curves. Consider again a big statistical sample of Earth-like planets having humanoid species at the same level of development that earthlings have now. That sample has one survivability curve, but we know nothing about it. So for lack of data, we make an educated estimate. The dashed red curve in this figure is the median of this estimate; the solid curves are the 2/3 confidence bounds. Outlying areas above and below the black curves each contain probability 1/6. The reason the curves level out with time is that the planet's civilizations have collapsed, which removes the threat from humanoid-made hazards.

4.11 Biases

Certain unavoidable assumptions and approximations in this treatise tend to overestimate or underestimate the threat. Here we collect and compare these. In this process we must avoid the temptation to emphasize individual hazards that are currently in the news and seem particularly threatening. Likewise, we must avoid emphasis on recent successes in overcoming threats. These factors belong in a bottom-up approach, Sec. 4.2. Since the top-down approach already transcends lists of hazards, defenses, and warnings, any mixing of the two can only lead to bias by duplication.

The published survival statistics used to substantiate the theory all consist of stage productions and business firms. These proxies (microcosms) have attributes in common with civilization and with humanity as a whole:

- All are exposed to many diverse hazards.
- Within each entity the individuals act from mixed motives that balance group interests against personal ones.
- All are aggregates of individuals, each of whom can be replaced while the entity remains intact.

- None of the entities (civilization, our species, business firms, stage productions) has a cutoff age, a maximum it cannot exceed.

However, there are two relevant differences:

- People in businesses and in theater work together for the common good and develop a sense of teamwork and group consciousness. This must have survival value, but it does not extend to humanity as a whole, which is too vast and amorphous for such feelings to take hold. This suggests that humanity may be less survivable than we infer from these proxies.
- People whose business fails expect to find another job. They will not fight for the business' survival with the same fierce determination that they fight for their life in those cases where they are aware of the threat in time to fight.

Let us include these two factors in a broader tally of mismatches between the assumptions and the mathematical model:

These two factors tend to overestimate the threat:

- The fierce determination mentioned above in comparison to our business proxies.
- The formulation recognizes only two calamities: extinction and civilization's collapse. Perhaps a sequence of lesser calamities would have a protective effect. Dinosaurs might have adapted to bolide strikes if small ones had occurred before the big one.

These four factors tend to underestimate the threat:

- Absence of teamwork compared to business proxies.
- For the parameter μ in Eq. 13 we used only two values, specifically 0.286 for ordinary hazards, Eq. 17, and 0.96 for digital tech, Eq. 20. However, there is actually a spread in values, and their effect is nonlinear, particularly values >1.0, which lead to a drop-dead pop-time. Discussion in *AW*, Appendix K.
- The concept of *unlimited survival* discussed in Sec. 4.1 is an ideal that is never fully met, and indeed all examples such as Fig. 8 show that the longest lived individuals, typically about 15%, exhibit some obsolescence and die off somewhat faster than the ideal rate. Humankind may fall in that 15%.
- Protection from some of the biggest hazards involves a political process, for example, enforcement of a treaty that protects us from climate change. This process proceeds at its characteristic pace. When the hazard rate exceeds that pace, it may overwhelm the defense. This compromises Eq. 11, which implies that hazard exposure is what counts, regardless of whether it is prolonged or compressed in time.

At this time I do not know how to modify the top-down analysis to reduce the biases listed above. Perhaps you can contribute. Meanwhile, another worthwhile task is to refine Eqs. 12 through 16, projecting future hazard exposure. This task requires analyzing a greater variety of statistics that indicate the growth of modern hazards, for example, the annual outlay for research in genetic engineering.

Chapter 5. Advice

Above all, *reassess your priorities and put long-term survival issues near the top. Keep tabs on developments in artificial intelligence (AI). Then, if and when the opportunity arises, support development of an AI overlord, or so-called AI Nanny.*

Be alert to indicators of serious trouble such as global warming, changes in the Black Sea, and whatever else might be man-made. Make a plan for the younger members of your family to join a survival colony or move somewhere that gives them a better chance.

An effective refuge will be expensive. If you are not wealthy, try to find a partner who is. *Encourage younger members of your family to acquire wealth.* Goods suitable for barter may be important. Timing may be crucial. Your money may be worthless if you hold it too long. Or you may spend too much on the wrong things if you buy too soon. Recall the gambler's song:[160]

> You've got to know when to hold 'em,
> Know when to fold 'em,
> Know when to walk away,
> Know when to run. ...

If you donate to charity, emphasize birth control, especially in the third world where your donation will produce maximum results. Forget endowing colleges and saving orangutans.

o—O—o

Make your elected representatives aware of important matters for national legislation that are not now on the political radar. These include ...

- License and regulate quants playing the stock market.
- Change tax laws to reduce extreme wealth. Begin government supervision of extreme private wealth, foreign as well as domestic. (Threats to humanity do not respect national boundaries.)
- Modify missile submarines, SSBNs, and their crews so that they double as survival habitats. The changes are modest, and they will at least double the chance that these boats serve a historic purpose.
- Support medium-term programs to develop earth-bound survival colonies. In particular, support ocean exploration to discover hydrothermal vents having potential for the survival scheme described in Section 3.2.3, Chapter 3.
- Support programs to develop survival colonies in space as soon as possible. In particular, consider Metzger's vision of a robotic industrial revolution that begins on the moon using lunar minerals for building material; see Chapter 3, Section 3.1. If this succeeds and grows exponentially it may lead to an artificial habitat such as O'Neill's cylinder to be launched from the moon.
- The preceding two items are very expensive, so oppose competing expensive programs that would divert funds. This includes all space missions beyond the moon, and especially any manned mission to Mars. One example of an unfortunate choice was the International Space Station.[161] It may be the most expensive artifact ever built at $150 billion. Likewise, be skeptical of big military projects and new weapons systems. The annual

budget of the US Department of Defense already exceeds the combined budgets of the next 17 biggest militaries.[162] Does the US really need more?

Laws should protect people from the next Carrington event, the solar flare of 1859 described in Section 2.1. This event will fry all electronics that are not well shielded. In particular, most new motor vehicles may stop or go out of control. Laws should require all new motor vehicles to provide a simple quick means to switch to fully manual control. (This also protects you from hackers messing with your driving.) I did not give this precaution a bullet in the list above because a Carrington disaster may be just the sort of unforgettable warning that could save the human race! Very likely it will happen during rush-hour traffic at some populated longitude, in which case stalled and wrecked vehicles may clog many urban roads.

o—O—o

Try to learn from doomsday preppers. Even if you dislike their subculture (hanging out at gun shows, for example), they may know things that could possibly save your life or your survival colony.

Join a group concerned with survival, for example the Lifeboat Foundation.

Finally, beware of pondering the apocalypse too intently. This is what can happen ...

Joke, this is merely a chandelier in the background at a party. (I never met the photographer; perhaps he saw an approximate alignment and then just for fun shifted his position to make it precise. The lovely lady on the right is Judith Strupp Wells, my wife, who cheerfully tolerates and even encourages my obsession with writing.)

Appendix A
Laplace's rule of succession

Think back to the old days when your daily news arrived as a physical newspaper tossed on your front yard. Suppose you have subscribed for 100 days during which you successfully found the paper 97 times. If you ask the probability that you find the paper tomorrow, you are inclined to estimate it as 97%, so you might think that the general formula for the probability of the next success after S successes in N trials is S/N. But suppose you have subscribed for only 3 days with 3 successes. Then the formula says that the probability of success tomorrow is 1.0, which cannot be correct.

Laplace's improved formula is

$$\text{Prob}(\text{next success} \mid N, S) = \frac{S+1}{N+2}$$

Then for the fourth day, the probability is only 4/5 = 80%. Immediately after you subscribe, $N = S = 0$, and the probability for the first morning is 1/2, which expresses your presumed complete ignorance about the time it takes the company to process your order. This formula can be derived from Bayesian theory,[163, 164] and if you have some knowledge of newspapers processing orders, then you can use Bayes to revise the "pseudo-counts" in the numerator and denominator.

Laplace's original example rule was the probability that the sun will rise tomorrow, a poor choice because astronomical orbits were already known. And so Laplace took needless flak for choosing a poor example.

Appendix B
Derivation of Gott's Predictor

Consider a random encounter between an entity and its observer. Assuming her arrival time is unbiased, the probability density for arrival is uniform, or in terms of integrated probability, she may arrive in the first half of the entity's duration with probability 1/2, or during the first third with probability 1/3, or

$$\text{Prob (arrival during the first fraction } X) = X. \qquad \text{(B-1)}$$

The sketch below shows a timeline in which the observer finds the entity's age is A and enquires about its future F or total duration $T = A + F$.

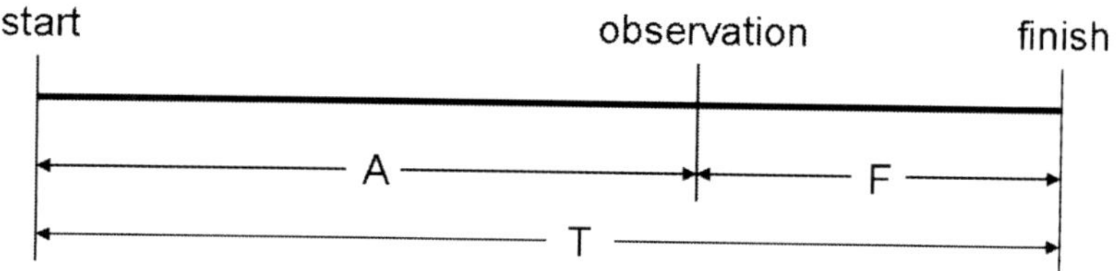

Gott's predictor is the probability that the observed entity will continue to survive for at least time F, which means that the observation occurs prior to $T - F$.

$$G(F) = \text{Prob(arrival prior to } T - F)$$

To apply the discussion above, express this in terms of a fraction.

$$G(F) = \text{Prob}\left(\text{arrival during first fraction } \frac{T-F}{T}\right)$$

Identify fraction (T-F)/F with X in Eq. A-1, and find

$$G(F) = \frac{T-F}{T} = \frac{A}{A+F} \qquad \text{(B-2)}$$

where the last step uses $T = A + F$. Eq. A-2 agrees with Eq. 2, as we set out to prove.

Appendix C
Initial survivability (life expectancy at birth)

Recall that $Q(T)$ denotes probability of an entity's survival (survivability) for at least time T measured from its outset (birth). In this appendix we derive Eq. 6 for Q by an alternate means that does not postulate a stream of observers. What follows is not a general proof of the formula, but rather a special case that appears likely to hold more generally.

Suppose that an entity has a known constant risk rate λ_0. This is the probability of its demise per unit time:

$$\lambda_0 = -\frac{1}{Q}\frac{dQ}{dt}$$

The well-known solution to this differential equation (DE) is

$$Q(t \mid \lambda_0) = \exp(-\lambda_0 t) \tag{C-1}$$

Next, suppose λ_0 is constant in time but differs among the specimens in a statistical sample. And suppose the density of specimens with any risk rate λ_0 is $F(\lambda_0)$. Then for the sample as a whole

$$Q(T) = \int_0^\infty F(\lambda_0) Q(T \mid \lambda_0)\, d\lambda_0 \tag{C-2}$$

Next, let us characterize $F(\lambda_0)$. A stage production rarely fails while the curtain is rising on opening night. A violent explosion or bolide would have to wreck the theater at that instant. Likewise, a business does not fail on opening day while its owner is unlocking the door to admit her first customers. Extremely high risk rates are very rare. We cannot define a sharp maximum cutoff for $F(\lambda_0)$, so let it be gradual; in other words, $F(\lambda_0) \to 0$ as $\lambda_0 \to \infty$. It turns out that Eq. 6 in the main text results when we assume the simplest possible decay function:

$$F(\lambda_0) = J \exp(-\lambda_0 J) \qquad \text{(C-3)}$$

This equation defines a parameter *J*. Another interpretation of *J* that is probably consistent with this one appears above Eq. 5 in the main text. I say "probably" because I have no insider information on businesses and stage productions that would substantiate the comparison.

Substituting Eqs. C-1 and C-3 into C-2 and integrating gives the desired result for survivability at time T:

$$Q(T) = \frac{J}{J+T} = \frac{1}{1+T/J} \qquad \text{(C-4)}$$

It may happen that a single hazard dominates the risk to every specimen in the statistical sample, in other words there is only one significant value of λ_0, but we don't know its value. In that case we reinterpret $F(\lambda_0)$ as the probability density of different values, and the same equations apply. Although this gives a best estimate of *Q*, "best" will not be very good because empirical statistics will better match Eq. 6 for the dominant value of λ_0, which we do not know.

For what it's worth, $Q(t)$ obeys the differential equation ...

$$dQ/dt = -Q^2/J \qquad \text{(C-5)}$$

Appendix D
Accelerating hazard rate

Since the pace of man-made hazards is accelerating rapidly, we investigate the case in which risk rate varies with time, $\lambda(t)$. The DE for Q and its well-known solution are a modification of the case in Appendix C:

$$\frac{dQ}{dt} = -Q\,\lambda(t) \qquad \text{and} \qquad Q(T) = \exp\left(-\int_0^T \lambda(t)\,dt\right) \qquad \text{(D-1)}$$

Let us express risk rate $\lambda(t)$ as the product of two factors, a constant vulnerability υ and a hazard exposure rate $z(t)$:

$$\lambda(t) = \upsilon\, z(t) \qquad \text{(D-2)}$$

For human survival z is some composite indicator of exposure to high-tech hazards: the number of published papers in science and engineering, gross world product, world population, and so forth; recall Figs. 11 & 14 and the discussions leading up to them. Vulnerability υ is an unknown constant multiplier that converts z to a risk rate, some probability of catastrophe per unit time.

Let Z denote the entity's cumulative exposure to hazards:

$$Z(T) = \int_0^T z(t)\,dt \qquad \text{(D-3)}$$

Substituting Eqs. D-2 & D-3 into D-1 gives

$$Q(t \mid v) = \exp(-v\,Z) \qquad \text{(D-4)}$$

Normally υ varies among individuals in the statistical sample or else is not known. In either case let $F(\upsilon)$ denote its probability density function (pdf):

$$Q(T) = \int_0^\infty F(v) Q(T|v)\, dv \tag{D-5}$$

As far as we know v is uniformly distributed. A convenient way to represent this is to use

$$F(v) = \varepsilon \exp(-\varepsilon \cdot v) \tag{D-6}$$

and eventually let $\varepsilon \to 0$. Substitute this in Eq. D-5 and integrate to obtain

$$Q(T) = \frac{\varepsilon}{\varepsilon + Z(T)} \tag{D-7}$$

Recall Eq. 7 from the main text:

$$Q(A+F) = Q(A) \times G(F|A) \tag{7}$$

To generalize Gott's predictor (Eq. 6) for the variable hazard case, solve Eq. 7 for G and evaluate the Qs using Eq. D-7:

$$G = \frac{Q(Z_p + Z_f)}{Q(Z_p)} = \lim \frac{\varepsilon + Z_p}{\varepsilon + Z_p + Z_f} = \frac{Z_p}{Z_p + Z_f} = \frac{1}{1 + Z_f / Z_p} \tag{D-8}$$

This is Eq. 11, the desired result.

Appendix E
Bivariate survivability

To my knowledge the multivariate survivability formulas, Eqs. 21 & 22 have no rigorous proof. To fill this gap, one should substantiate the formula using survival statistics for entities subject to dual cum-risks, one of which is not time. We prefer that the statistical records state the cause of each demise so that we can fit the formula to multiple equations, one for the "dead body count" due to each hazard; see *AW* Appendix G. Let us call this a *strong substantiation.*

If we were compiling vital statistics, we could easily obtain strong substantiation, namely mortality data disaggregated by cause of death. All we would need is a stack of death certificates. However, for our class of entities, the unlimited survivors, statistics listing causes are surprisingly scarce. Without them we can still get a *weak substantiation* by adjusting all parameters to find the best fit to the single multivariate equation for the overall survivability, i.e. factors like Eq. 21, but probably only 2 or 3 of them. If the resulting set of parameters is both plausible and unique (only one best fit), we then have reasonable assurance that the formulation is working.

We do have one example, unfortunately the weak kind, but to some extent the size of the statistical sample makes up for the weakness. The results are plausible, unique, and surprisingly consistent using two different criteria for data selection. The entities are stage productions, the risks are of two types, those that depend on the overall duration T and the overall number of performances S (for shows). Survivability declines with S simply because many performances deplete the supply of people willing to travel to the theater and pay admission. Excessive duration T also stresses a stage production. One with frequent hiatuses fails to provide steady employment for the cast and staff and steady use of the stage and props. Hence, startup costs recur with each revival. In the long haul, public tastes change or events in the news redirect public interest or sometimes make the topic distasteful.

The most complete and readily available statistics apply to the London Stage.[165] This source gives the opening date, the closing date, and the total number of performances, in other words survivability from the opening, not from some observed age, and so we convert from the G form in Eq. 21 back to the Q form as in Eq. 6 with new notation appropriate to stage productions, namely T and S:

$$Q = \left(\frac{J}{J+T}\right)^{q} \times \left(\frac{K}{K+S}\right)^{k} \qquad \text{(E-1)}$$

Appendix H in *AW* describes a regression analysis to determine the parameters J, K, k, and q. Since this expression evolved by factoring Gott's predictor, we expect that

$$k + q = 1.0 \qquad \text{(E-2)}$$

but this argument is not a rigorous proof. Hence, I let each exponent vary independently and let the regression analysis discover that the best fit occurs when their sum is very nearly 1.0.

o—O—o

The statistical ensemble consists of 379 shows first performed in London during the five years 1920 to 1924, a period chosen to avoid both World Wars and the

Spanish influenza. Figure E shows a scatter diagram of each production's performances and durations. Most of them fall on or near the straight brown line, which denotes eight performances per week, typically six evenings and two matinees. The few shows to the upper left of the brown line in the diagram played twice per day during at least part of their run.

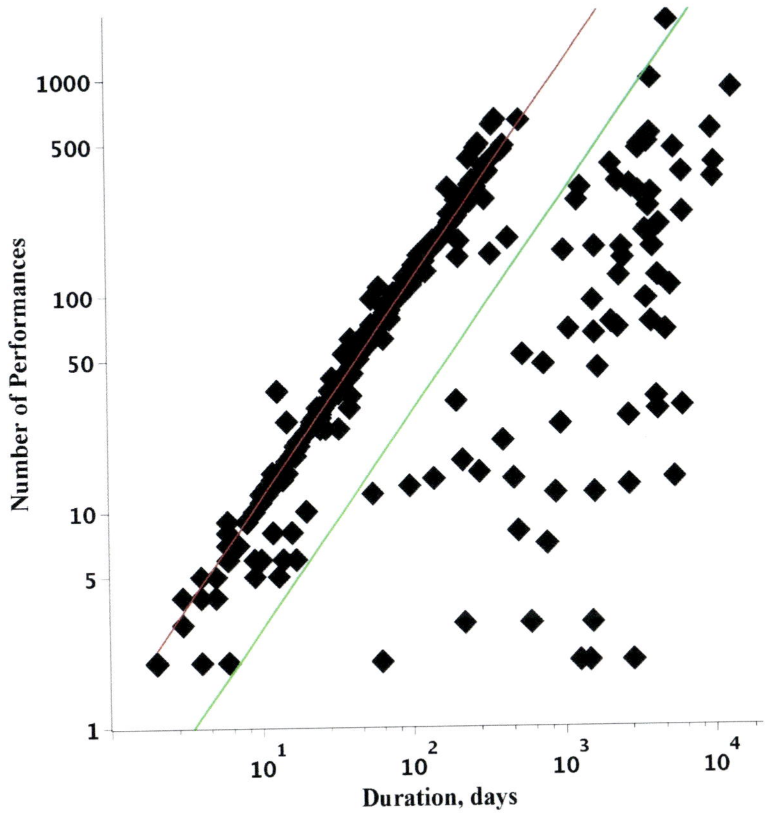

Figure E. Scatter diagram for London shows number of performances versus duration

The green line represents an average of two performances per week. I chose this number somewhat arbitrarily to set apart the 69 shows to the lower right (22% of the total) that have lengthy hiatuses. In some cases a brief run is an annual event, sometimes during the holiday season. Let us call this group the *occasional shows* and treat them as an entity distinct from the majority in the *main sequence* to the upper left. Perhaps each occasional show has a small but devoted following of people who expect to attend it repeatedly, as many opera and ballet fans do.

In the main sequence S is more or less proportional to T, namely $S = 8T/7$. Substitute this in Eq. E-1 and put K = 8L/7, and the equation takes the form

$$Q = \left(\frac{J}{J+T}\right)^q \times \left(\frac{L}{L+T}\right)^k \qquad \text{(E-3)}$$

This has univariate form, only T, which is a step closer to the original Gott's predictor, and so we do not expect trouble, and indeed regression analysis gives $q = 0.081$, $k = 0.643$, and

$$q + k = 0.945$$

which is certainly close enough to 1.0. As expected, the number of performances consumes survivability much faster than the passage of time. Assuming the true values of q & k total 1.0, they are about

$$q = 0.1, \quad k = 0.9$$

The occasional shows, which concern us more, by luck give an even better result: $q = 0.370$, $k = 0.643$, and

$$q + k = 1.013$$

For these shows, performances still have the greater statistical weight, but not so dominant, probably because occasional shows tend to be compositions that people see repeatedly, e.g. Tchaikovsky's *Nutcracker*

Suite. In short, the whole formulation seems quite plausible and explicable.

One final note: Recall that the two factors in Equation E-1 derive from the product rule: if X and Y are *statistically independent*, then the probability of both equals the probability of X *times* the probability of Y. One might think that the strong correlation between performances and duration along the main sequence would violate the requirement for independence, but this is not the case. The kind of independence that the product rule requires is that the *hazards* against performances (for example audience depletion) are unrelated to the *hazards* against duration (for example revival startup costs). The product rule does not exclude schedule synchronization, which is a different sort of dependence.

Appendix F
Probability tutorial

Recall the simplistic rules for probability: logical OR means to add probabilities; logical AND means multiply providing the two events are statistically independent.

Suppose you have three dice that appear identical. Two of them are fair, but one is loaded so that the probability of rolling six with it is 1/3. You pick a die at random and roll it. What is the probability of getting six?

The probability of choosing a fair die AND rolling six is the product:

$$\frac{2}{3}\times\frac{1}{6}=\frac{1}{9}$$

Similarly the probability of choosing the loaded die AND rolling six is

$$\frac{1}{3}\times\frac{1}{3}=\frac{1}{9}$$

However, our question does not inquire about the die, it can be fair OR loaded. Hence, we take the sum:

$$\text{Probability of six } =\frac{1}{9}+\frac{1}{9}=\frac{2}{9}=22\% \qquad \text{(F-1)}$$

which compares to 17% for a fair die. In other words, we have AND embedded in ORs and therefore take the sum of the products.

This dice example applies to discrete probability. Our case involves a continuous probability density function (pdf) as follows.

o—O—o

In Eq. 25 we have a survivability formula $G(x,q,v)$ that is a function of pop-time x and two statistical weights q & v. Here we are not concerned with x, only q & v, which occur with probability density $W(q,v)$ given by Eqs. 26 & 29. The survivability as a function of x alone without regard to q & v is analogous to Eq. F-1 above except that the sum becomes an integration because q & v are continuous:

$$G(x) = \iint G(x,q,v) \times W(q,v)\, dq\, dv \qquad \text{(F-2)}$$

where it is understood that the integration extends over the permissible area shown in Fig. 15.

Appendix G
Details of pdf for civilization's survival

Equation 28 in the text gives mean values for the three statistical weights. Two of them, q & v, were found by the normal formula from basic probability theory of continuous random variables. Let angle brackets denote mean, z denote either q or v, and W the pdf. Then the formula for the mean is ...

$$\langle z \rangle = \int_0^1 \int_0^1 z \cdot W(q,v)\, dq\, dv \qquad \text{(G-1)}$$

Likewise, the formula for mean value of the third st-wt, $n = 1 - q - v$, is

$$\langle n \rangle = \int_0^1 \int_0^1 (1 - q - v) \cdot W(q,v)\, dq\, dv \qquad \text{(G-2)}$$

By adding the integrands of the three means, it is apparent that

$$\langle q \rangle + \langle v \rangle + \langle n \rangle = \int_0^1 \int_0^1 W(q,v)\, dq\, dv = 1.0 \qquad \text{(G-3)}$$

Double integrations may be performed in either sequence. Some of them can be analytic, but making them all numerical is simpler and lets the software decide what sequence works best for it.

Appendix H
Risk rate for survival

By definition rate of loss is the risk rate times the amount surviving:

$$-\frac{dG}{dt} = R \cdot G \text{, hence}$$

$$R = -\frac{1}{G}\frac{dG}{dt} = -\frac{d}{dt}(\ln G) \qquad \text{(H-1)}$$

Let us use the notation for civilization's survival and rewrite Eq. 25 as

$$G = \left(\frac{406 + x}{406}\right)^{-2.4q} \cdot \left(\frac{556 + x}{556}\right)^{-25v} \qquad \text{(H-2)}$$

Quantities inside the parentheses have units of billions of people years, BPY. *G* depends on time through *x(t)*, Eq. 14. In calculus notation it becomes

$$x(t) = \int^{t} p(u)\, du \quad \text{and then} \quad \frac{dx}{dt} = p(t) \qquad \text{(H-3)}$$

where *p* is world population as a function of time.

For Eq. H-1 we need the natural logarithm of Eq. H-2:

$$-\ln G = 2.4\, q[\ln(406 + x) - \ln 406] + 25\, v[\ln(556 + x) - \ln 556]$$

and then the differentiation in Eq. H-1 using H-3 gives

$$R = p \cdot \left(\frac{2.4q}{406 + x} + \frac{25v}{556 + x}\right) \qquad \text{(H-4)}$$

In the text we emphasize expected value of the initial risk rate. Putting x = 0, and p = 7.3 billion gives

$$\langle R(x = 0)\rangle = (4.3\langle q\rangle + 33\langle v\rangle)\,\%/\text{year} \qquad \text{(H-5)}$$

Appendix I
The spread in civilization's survivability

Recall our formula for the survivability of civilization, namely

$$G_{civ} = \left(\frac{1}{1+x/406}\right)^{2.4q} \times \left(\frac{1}{1+x/526}\right)^{25v} \qquad (25)$$

x = future pop-time

Here q and v are unknown parameters whose probabilities are described by the following pdf:

$$W_{civ} = \begin{cases} \frac{20.88}{\sqrt{v}} \times (1-q-v)^2 \times (q-v), & \text{inside the triangle} \\ 0, & \text{outside} \end{cases} \qquad (26)$$

Here "triangle" refers to Fig. 15 ...

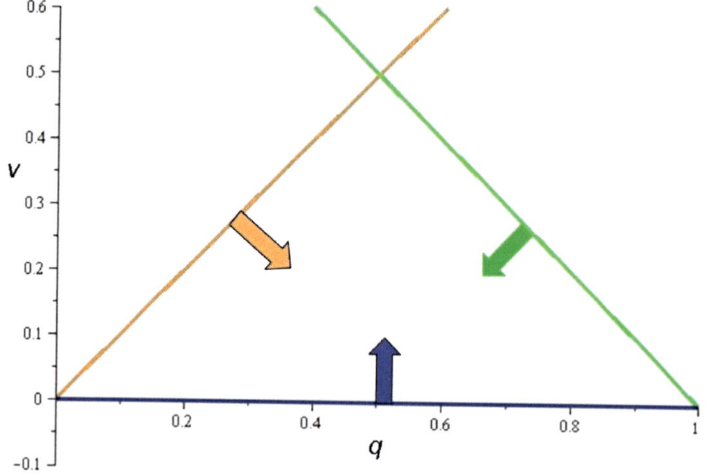

Fig. 15. Permissible area in the q,v plane

We need a formal mathematical means to define "inside the triangle," for which we define a unit wedge:

$$H(x) = \begin{cases} x, & x > 0 \\ 0, & \mathrm{x} \leq 0 \end{cases} \tag{I-1}$$

Using this, Eq. 26 becomes

$$W_{civ} = \frac{20.88}{\sqrt{v}} \times H[(1-q-v)]^2 \times H(q-v) \tag{I-2}$$

Recall the contour plot of this pdf, Fig. 16 in the text:

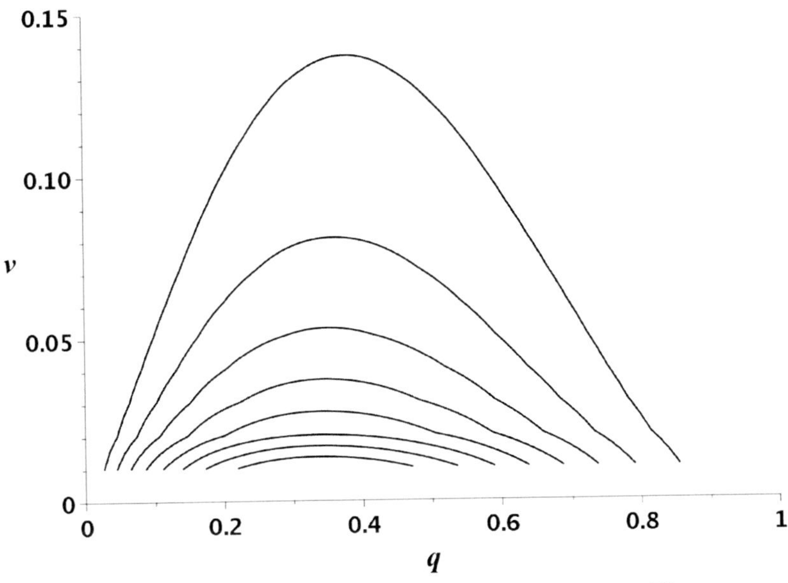

Fig. 16. Pdf for civilization's survivability

o—O—o

Let U denote the unit step function

$$U(x) = \begin{cases} 1, & x > 0 \\ 0, & \mathrm{x} \leq 0 \end{cases} \tag{I-3}$$

and consider the expression

$$Prob = \int_0^{1/2} \int_0^1 U(C - G_{civ}) \cdot W_{civ} \, dq \, dv \tag{I-4}$$

Everywhere in the q,v plane that the contour level C exceeds survivability G, the factor $U = 1.0$. Likewise, the integrand vanishes everywhere that $C < G_{civ}$. Thus Eq. I-4 integrates all the probability in the u,v plane for which the survivability does not exceed the given contour C. By performing many such integrals and interpolating among the data, I developed the integrated probabilities required to plot the survivability curves in Fig. 17:

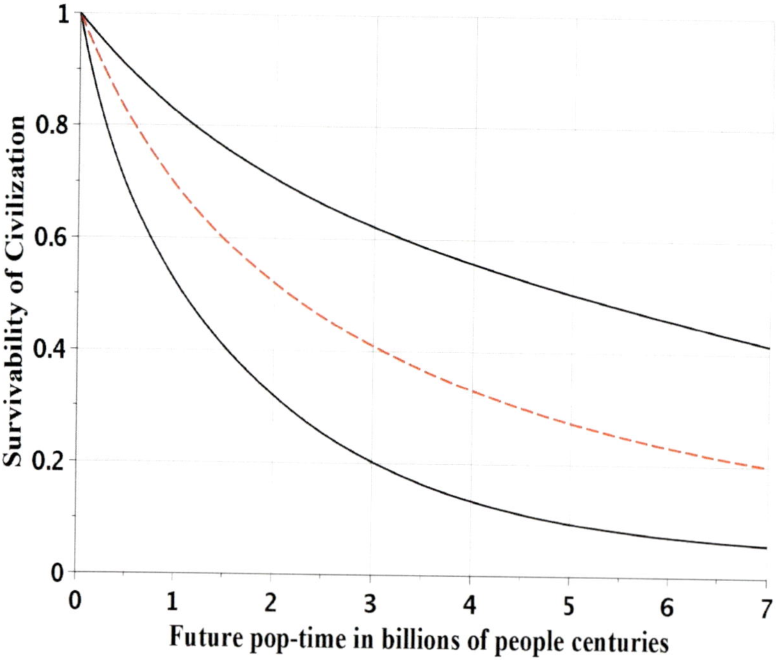

Fig. 17. Probability of civilization's survival as a function of future population-time in billions of people-centuries

Appendix J
Extinction conditioned by civilization's collapse

I resolved not to put any calculus in the main text, which is why the text does not show a final formula for survivability of humankind corresponding to Eq. 25 for civilization. Instead, the main text shows Eq. 33 for mortality rate. The probability of extinction, Fig. 19 reproduced below, is simply the integral of mortality. Let us call it X for extinction, and let z denote a dummy variable of integration for intermediate values of x. Thus the deferred formula is ...

$$X = \int_0^x \left(\frac{2.4r}{406+z} + \frac{25u}{556+z} \right) \cdot \left(\frac{1}{1+z/406} \right)^{2.4q} \cdot \left(\frac{1}{1+z/556} \right)^{25v} dz$$

(J-1)

Parameters r, u, q, and v are random statistical weights described by the pdf in Expression 32. Let us rewrite this pdf using the unit step and wedge functions defined in Appendix I:

$$U(x) = \begin{cases} 1, & x > 0 \\ 0, & x \le 0 \end{cases} \qquad H(x) = \begin{cases} x, & x > 0 \\ 0, & x \le 0 \end{cases}$$

$$W_{hum} = \frac{[H(1-q-v)]^6 \cdot H(q-v) \cdot H(r-u) \cdot H(q-r) \cdot U(v-u)}{\sqrt{u \cdot v}}$$

(J-2)

In the case of civilization's survival we integrated the probability outside contours in the q,v plane to get the median and its surrounding limits for 1/6 and 5/6 probability. Next we need the corresponding quantity in the four-dimensional q,v,r,u hyperplane:

$$\int_0^{1/2}\int_0^{1}\int_0^{1/2}\int_0^{1} U(C-X)\cdot W_{hum}\, dq\, dv\, dr\, du \qquad \text{(J-3)}$$

By performing this integral for many combinations of x and C, I was able to interpolate points needed to plot the curves in Fig. 19 reproduced here.

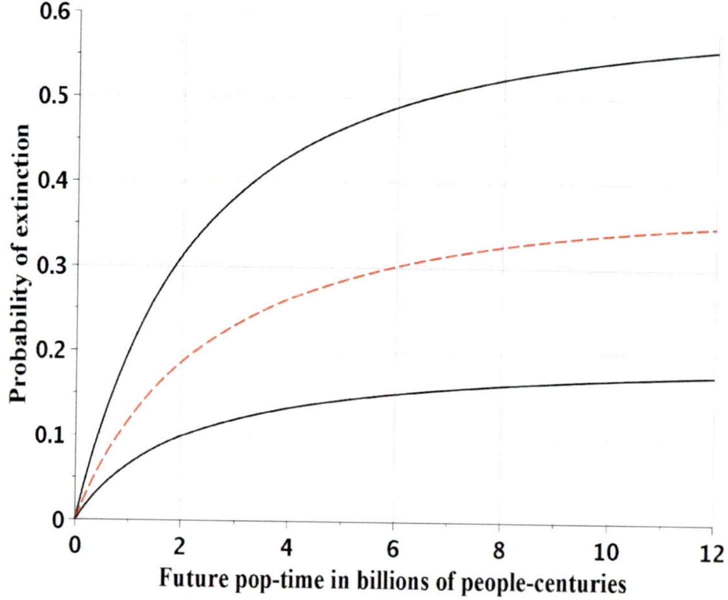

Fig. 19. Probability of human extinction as a function of future population-time in billions of people-centuries

Evaluation of Eq. J-3 was an arduous task, a five-dimensional integration in q,v,r,u,z space. Four dimensions are explicit in Eq. J-3, and the fifth is implicit in X; see Eq. J-1. I was barely able to do this by upgrading my computer to 8 GB of memory and purchasing sophisticated math software, namely Maple 2016. I spent hours on the telephone to Maple tech support, where Boris was most patient. Maple lets me trade off accuracy for reduced integration time; although the accuracy was still more than adequate for our purpose. Evidently it examines the 5-D space on a course grid to pick out hyper volumes that contribute most to the result. Then it focuses on those volumes to refine the result.

References and Notes

1 Martin Rees, *Our Final Century: Will the Human Race Survive the Twenty-first Century?*, Arrow Books Ltd., 2004.

2 Stephen Hawking, http://bigthink.com/videos/abandon-earth-or-face-extinction, http://abcnews.go.com/blogs/technology/2011/11/stephen-hawking-human-survival-depends-on-settling-space.

3 John Derbyshire, *We Are Doomed: Reclaiming Conservative Pessimism*, Crown Forum, Random House, New York, 2009.

4 John Derbyshire, *Prime Obsession: Bernhard Riemann and the Greatest Unsolved Problem in Mathematics*, Penguin Books, New York, 2004.

5 John Leslie, *The End of the World: The Science and Ethics of Human Extinction*, Routledge, London 1996.

6 Naomi Klein, *This Changes Everything: Capitalism vs. the Climate*, Simon & Schuster, 2014.

7 Charles Perrow, *Normal Accidents: Living with High Risk Technologies*, Basic Books, 1984.

8 See endnotes 1, 5, 9, 10, 59. Additional books:

- John Casti, *X-Events: the Collapse of Everything*, William Morrow / HarperCollins, New York, 2012. Here *X* denotes extreme.
- Annalee Newitz, *Scatter, Adapt, and Remember*, Doubleday, 2013. Interestingly Newitz has summarized her advice in her title.
- Fred Guterl, *The Fate of the Species: Why the human race may cause its own extinction and How we can stop it*,

Bloomsbury, New York, 2012. Guterl is executive editor of *Scientific American.* Unfortunately he forgot to include how we can prevent extinction.

- Richard A. Posner, *Catastrophe: Risk and Response*, Oxford U. Press, New York, 2004. Posner is a judge of the U.S. Court of Appeals and prolific author. He emphasizes some risks that are actually quite negligible: asteroid strikes (see Chapter 1.1) and particle-accelerator disaster (see 1.8.7). The book is quite dull, and the font in Oxford's paperback edition is small and faint, and words often divide only two letters from the end of the line.
- David Mills, *Our Uncertain Furure: When Digital Evolution, Global Warming, and Automation Converge*, Pacific Beach Publishing, 2013. This is an optimistic view. "Many different predictions appeared recently, most mutually exclusive."
- James R. Chiles, *Inviting Disaster: Lessons from the Edge of Technology*, HarperBusiness, 2001. Case studies without overarching analysis. Selected chapter subtitles reveal the flavor: When flagship projects run out of time; Testing is such a bother; Go away, I'm busy.

9 Nick Bostrom, Milan M. Ćirković, *Global Catastrophic Risks*, Oxford U. Press, 2008.

10 Willard Wells, Apocalypse When?, Springer & Praxis, Chichester, UK, 2009. Frequently cited herein as *AW* for short.

11 "Human Extinction Isn't That Unlikely," The Atlantic, April 29, 2016, https://www.yahoo.com/news/human-extinction-isnt-unlikely-143313610.html.

[12] London Futurists, Lead editor David W. Wood, Anticipating 2025, Amazon Digital Services (Kindle), 2014.

[13] Stuxnet, Wikipedia.

[14] Ben Goertzel, Wikipedia.

[15] Does Humanity Need an AI Nanny?, Humanity+ Magazine, August 17, 2011, http://hplusmagazine.com/2011/08/17/does-humanity-need-an-ai-nanny.

[16] Genetic Programming, Wikipedia.

[17] David L. Poole & Alan K. Mackworth, *Artificial Intelligence*, Cambridge U. Press, 2010. Also available at http://artint.info/html/ArtInt.html. Excellent reviews.

[18] Keith Frankish & William M. Ramsey, *The Cambridge Handbook of Artificial Intelligence*, Cambridge U. Press, 2014.

[19] Kevin Warwick, *Artificial Intelligence: The Basics*, Routledge, 2011.

[20] Jeff Heaton, *Artificial Intelligence for Humans*, http://www.amazon.com/s/ref=series_rw_dp_labf?_encoding=UTF8&field-collection=Artificial%20Intelligence%20for%20Humans&url=search-alias%3Ddigital-text.

[21] Lifeboat Foundation, AIShield, https://lifeboat.com/ex/ai.shield.

[22] Michael Anissimov, presentation at *Global Catastrophic Risks & Radical Futures*, conference by Brighter Brains Institute, Piedmont, CA, June 14, 2014.

[23] List of artificial intelligence projects, Wikipedia.

[24] Faraday Cage, Wikipedia.

25 No-Lone Zone, Wikipedia: Two-man rule, Section 3.

26 Dog, Wikipedia.

27 Ian Pearson, "Benign AI" https://lifeboat.com/blog/2015/02/benign-ai.

28 Matthias Scheutz, Chapter 12 in The Cambridge Handbook of Artificial Intelligence, Cambridge U. Press, Aug. 2014, eds: Keith Frankish & William M. Ramsey.

29 "2001: A Space Odyssey" (film), Wikipedia.

30 Ray Kurzweil, Wikipedia.

31 Ray Kurzweil, *The Age of Spiritual Machines: When Computers Exceed Human Intelligence,* Viking Press, 1999, ISBN 0-670-88217-8 and *The Singularity Is Near*, Viking, 2005, ISBN 978-0-670-03384-3.

32 Functional neuroimaging, Wikipedia; see also Neuroimaging, Wikipedia.

33 Gabriele Gratton & Monica Fabiani, "Shedding light on brain function: the event-related optical signal," *Trends in Cognitive Sciences*, vol.5 pp. 357–63 (1 Aug 2001).

34 Stuxnet, Wikipedia.

35 Marc Goodman, *Future Crimes: Everything is connected, Everyone is vulnerable, and What We Can Do about it,* Chapter 8, Doubleday, 2015.

36 VirusBlokAda, Wikipedia.

37 David Brin warned of quants via a private channel.

38 Again, thanks to David Brin.

39 Marc Goodman, *Future Crimes*, Chapter 16, Doubleday 2015.

40 Nina Golgowski, *Daily Mail*, 23 April 2013, UK, http://www.dailymail.co.uk/news/article-2313652/AP-

Twitter-hackers-break-news-White-House-explosions-injured-Obama.html.

41 "An alternative to high-frequency trading," Capital Ideas magazine, U. Chicago, Booth. School of Business, Fall 2013, http://www.chicagobooth.edu/capideas/magazine/fall-2013/high-frequency-trading.

42 James Barrat, *Our Final Invention: Artificial Intelligence and the End of the Human Era,* St. Martin's Press, New York, 2013.

43 Nick Bostrom, *Superintelligece: Paths, Dangers, Strategies,* Oxford U. Press, 2014.

44 Eliezer Yudkowsky, Section 15.10, p. 331, in "Artificial Intelligence as a positive and negative factor in global risk," Chapter 15 in *Global Catastrophic Risks* edited by Bostrom & Ćirković, Oxford U. Press, 2008.

45 Stuart Armstrong, *Smarter Than Us: the Rise of Machine Intelligence*, Machine Intelligence Research Institute, Berkeley, 2014, Kindle, ISBN 193931108X.

46 Ben Goertzel, "Saving the World with Analytical Philosophy," http://hplusmagazine.com/2014/02/28/saving-the-world-with-analytical-philosophy.

47 Stuart Armstrong, Anders Sandberg, & Nick Bostrom, "Thinking inside the box: using and controlling an Oracle AI." http://www.nickbostrom.com/papers/oracle.pdf. An apparently older version is at http://www.aleph.se/papers/oracleAI.pdf.

48 Louis A. Del Monte, *The Artificial Intelligence Revolution: Will Artificial Intelligence Serve Us or Replace Us?*, Amazon Digital Services, 2014.

49 Ted Chu, *Human Purpose and Transhuman Potential: A Cosmic Vision of our Future Evolution*, Origin Press, 2014.

50 BioShield, Lifeboat Foundation, BioShield, https://lifeboat.com/ex/bio.shield.

51 InternetShield, Lifeboat Foundation, https://lifeboat.com/ex/internet.shield.

52 Solar Storm of 1859, Wikipedia.

53 Toba Catastrophe theory, Wikipedia; see also Supervolcano, Wikipedia.

54 Michael Anissimov, Classifying Existential Risks, https://lifeboat.com/ex/classifying.extinction.risks (2007).

55 "Developing Early Warning Systems for Killer Asteroids," *Discover* magazine, Sept. 2013, http://discovermagazine.com/2013/september/17-hunting-season-for-asteroids#.Ui0XnH_HC8B.

56 Chelyabinsk Meteor, Wikipedia.

57 Clara Moskowitz, "U.N. Heeds Astronaut Advice on Shielding Earth from Asteroids," *Scientific American*, Jan. 16, 2014. http://www.scientificamerican.com/article.cfm?id=un-heeds-astronaut-advice-on-shielding-earth-from-asteroids.

58 Black Sea Scene, http://www.blackseascene.net/content/content.asp?menu=0040032_000000.

59 Peter Ward, *Under a Green Sky*, HarperCollins, New York, 2007.

60 Black Sea, Wikipedia.

61 Yellowstone Caldera, Wikipedia.

62 Hsin-Hua Huang, et al, "The Yellowstone magmatic system from the mantle plume to the upper crust," Science, vol. 348, 15 May 2015.

63 Robert G. Edwards, http://www.bioethicsanddisability.org/Writinogonthewall.htm.

64 Abortion in the United States, Wikipedia; see Section 2, History.

65 Abraham Maslow, "A Theory of Human Motivation," *Psychological Review*, v.50, pp. 370–96, 1943. See also Maslow's hierarchy of needs, Wikipedia.

66 Michael Anissimov, First-Stage Nanoproducts and Nanoweaponry, https://lifeboat.com/ex/nanoweaponry (2006).

67 David Brin, *The Transparent Society,* Perseus Books, 1998, ISBN 0-7382-0144-8.

68 Robert A. Freitas, "Molecular Manufacturing: Too Dangerous to Allow?," https://lifeboat.com/ex/molecular.manufacturing.

69 K. Eric Drexler, *Engines of Creation: The Coming Era of Nanotechnology,* Anchor Press/Doubleday, New York, 1986. See: http://e-drexler.com/p/06/00/EOC_Cover.html.

70 Robert A. Freitas, Some Limits to Global Ecophagy by Biovorous Nanoreplicators, with Public Policy Recommendations, https://lifeboat.com/ex/global.ecophagy.

71 Locust, Wikipedia.

72 "Regeneration in Planaria," Phillip A Newmark & Alejandro Sánchez Alvarado, 2001, Encyclopedia of Life Sciences, Nature Publishing Group,

http://planaria.neuro.utah.edu/publications/PN_ELS01.pdf.

73 Antarctic Krill, Wikipedia.

74 A. Atkinson, V. Siegel, E. A. Pakhomov, M. H. Jessopp, V. Loeb, "A re-appraisal of the total biomass and annual production of Antarctic krill," *Deep-Sea Research I* **56**, pp. 727–740, http://www.iced.ac.uk/documents/Atkinson%20et%20al,%20Deep%20Sea%20Research%20I,%202009.pdf (2009).

75 Iron Fertilization, Wikipedia.

76 "Bill Gates warns that a devastating pandemic is right around the corner." The Huffington Post, Feb. 18, 2017. http://newscdn.newsrep.net/h5/nrshare.html?r=3&lan=en_US&pid=24&id=o090d3bd9q9_us&app_lan=&mcc=310&declared_lan=en_US&pubaccount=ocms_0&referrer=200620&showall=1&mcc=310

77 Great Oxygenation Event, Wikipedia.

78 Emmanuel Saez & Gabriel Zucman, Wealth Inequality in the United States since 1913, slide presentation Oct. 2014, http://gabriel-zucman.eu/files/SaezZucman2014Slides.pdf.

79 Robert Durst, Wikipedia.

80 Henry Fountain, "A Rogue Climate Experiment Outrages Scientists," New York Times, http://www.nytimes.com/2012/10/19/science/earth/iron-dumping-experiment-in-pacific-alarms-marine-experts.html.

81 Edward Fischer, Our Western civilization itself is a bubble, Interview with Arthur Demarest, http://www.pbs.org/newshour/making-sense/indiana-

jones-collapsed-cultures-western-civilization-bubble, December 22, 2014.

82 "Zombie Creatures: What happens when animals are possessed by a parasitic puppet master?," *Scientific American*, http://www.scientificamerican.com/slideshow/zombie-creatures-parasites.

83 Eliot Barford, "Parasite makes mice lose fear of cats permanently," *Nature, International weekly journal of science*, 18 September 2013, http://www.nature.com/news/parasite-makes-mice-lose-fear-of-cats-permanently-1.13777.

84 Survivalism, Wikipedia.

85 Tristan da Cunha, Wikipedia.

86 Murray-McIntosh, R. P., Scrimshaw, B. J., Hatfield, P. J., & Penny, D. (1998). "Testing migration patterns and estimating founding population size in Polynesia by using human mtDNA sequences," *Proceedings of National Academy of Science USA*, *95*(15), 9047–9052.
Jody Hey, (2005). On the number of new world founders: A population genetic portrait of the peopling of the Americas. *PLoS Biology*, *3*(6), 965–975.

87 Q&A: Frozen sperm, BBC News, 25 May 2004, http://news.bbc.co.uk/2/hi/health/3745085.stm.

88 P. Metzger, et al, "Affordable, Rapid Bootstrapping of the Space Industry and Solar System Civilization, *J. of Aerospace Engineering*, v. 26, Special issue: In Situ Resource Utilization, pp. 18–29, 2013.

89 Gerald K. O'Neill, "The Colonization of Space," *Physics Today*, v.27, pp. 32–40, 1974.

90 G. K. O'Neill, *The High Frontier: Human colonies in space*, William Morrow, N.Y., 1977.

91 O'Neill cylinder, Wikipedia.

92 Brian Wang, David Brin, and probably others.

93 Ship-Submarine Recycling Program, Wikipedia.

94 "Russia's Nuclear Leftovers," http://jonbowermaster.com/blog/2009/05/russias-nuclear-leftovers.

95 Ohio-class submarine, Wikipedia.

96 The first was the USS *Nautilus* launched in 1954.

97 HMS Conqueror (S48), Wikipedia.

98 "The Opposition of Mars," http://science.nasa.gov/science-news/science-at-nasa/2014/28mar_opposition.

99 Suggested by David Brin of Lifeboat Foundation.

100 Carl Engelking, Fake astronauts move into simulated Mars colony on Hawaii Volcano, April 3, 2014, http://blogs.discovermagazine.com/d-brief/2014/04/03/fake-astronauts-move-into-simulated-mars-colony-on-hawaii-volcano/#.U0nfN6LJGuO.

101 "Hawaii Space Exploration Analog and Simulation," http://hi-seas.org.

102 Mars-500, Wikipedia.

103 Mars Society, Wikipedia.

104 "MA365, a One-Year Mars Simulation in the Canadian Arctic," http://www.indiegogo.com/projects/ma365-a-one-year-mars-simulation-in-the-canadian-arctic.

105 Hydrothermal Vents, Woods Hole Oceanographic Institution, http://www.whoi.edu/main/topic/hydrothermal-vents.

106 Hydrothermal Vent, Wikipedia.

107 Kristin Ludwig, Deborah Kelley, "Formation of Carbonate Chimneys at the Lost City Hydrothermal Field," *Ocean Explorer*, NOAA 2005. http://oceanexplorer.noaa.gov/explorations/05lostcity/background/chimney/chimney.html.

108 East Pacific Vent at 9°N, 2,600 meters on Tube Worm Pillar. Giant tubeworms close up with vent fish. http://archive.noc.ac.uk/chess/event/galapagos_event.php.

109 Taro, Wikipedia, Section 2, Toxicity.

110 Cassava, Wikipedia.

111 Inuit Diet, Wikipedia, Section 3, Nutrition.

112 Aquarius Underwater Laboratory, http://oceanexplorer.noaa.gov/technology/diving/aquarius/aquarius.html.

113 Ben Hellwarth, Sea Base Alpha, *Discover* magazine, June 2012, pp. 33–9 & 66.

114 James W. Miller & Ian G. Koblick, *Living and Working in the Sea*, Best Publishing Co., 2nd edition, Dec. 1995, ISBN 1886699011.

115 University Of Washington. "Quake Jars Assumptions About Crustal Plumbing, Life At Mid-Ocean Ridges," Science Daily, 21 September 2000. http://www.sciencedaily.com/releases/2000/09/000921072840.htm.

116 Gerardo Hiriart, et al, "Submarine Geothermics; Hydrothermal Vents and Electricity Generation," *Proceedings World Geothermal Congress 2010*, Bali, Indonesia, April 2010, http://www.slideshare.net/jjsoto00/submarine-

geothermics-hydrothermal-vents-and-electricity-generation.

117 Willard Wells, "The Case for Survival Colonies: Soliciting Colonists," Special Report, Lifeboat Foundation, https://lifeboat.com/ex/case.for.survival.colonies.

118 Lifeboat Foundation, LifeShield Bunkers, https://lifeboat.com/ex/life.shield.bunkers#participation.

119 Doomsday Preppers, Wikipedia.

120 Luxury Survival Condo, http://www.survivalcondo.com.

121 D. C. Stewart, Postapocalypse Condominiums, *Discover* magazine, June 2012, pp. 14–15.

122 Silo Cutaway, http://search.yahoo.com/search?p=larry+hall+kansas+silo&ei=UTF-8&fr=chrf-yff19.

123 "Vivos Indiana," http://www.terravivos.com/secure/indiana.htm.

124 Bill Draper, "Developer: Kansas caverns could preserve human race," http://news.yahoo.com/developer-kan-caverns-could-preserve-human-race-071249444.html, *Associated Press*, 2014.

125 "Silohome," http://www.silohome.com/index.htm.

126 Fermi Paradox, Wikipedia.

127 List of Major Power Outages, Wikipedia.

128 Too Big to Fail, Wikipedia; see Section 4.3 Too big to fail tax.

129 Bradley Morton & Brian Kierland, "How to predict future duration from present age," *The Philosophical Quarterly*, Vol 56, #222, pp. 16–38.

130 Donella H. Meadows, *et al*: *Limits to Growth*, Potomac Associates, New York, 1972, and *The 30-year Update*, Chelsea Green Publishing Co., 2004.

131 Mihajlo D. Mesarovic, *Mankind at the Turning Point*, E. P. Dutton (Nov. 1974), http://www.amazon.com/Mankind-Turning-Point-Second-Report/dp/0525039457.

132 Club of Rome, Wikipedia.

133 Safa Motesharrei, Jorge Rivas, & Eugenia Kalnay, "Human and Nature Dynamics (HANDY): Modeling Inequality and Use of Resources in the Collapse or Sustainability of Societies," *Ecological Economics*, http://www.sciencedirect.com/science/article/pii/S0921800914000615.

134 Stephen Luntz, *IFL Science*, March 19, 2014, http://www.iflscience.com/environment/according-nasa-funded-study-were-pretty-much-screwed.

135 Huffpost Tech, UK, Mar. 17, 2014, http://www.huffingtonpost.co.uk/2014/03/17/civilisation-doomed_n_4977387.html.

136 Nafeez Ahmed, "NASA-funded study: industrial civilization headed for 'irreversible collapse'?" The Guardian, http://www.theguardian.com/environment/earth-insight/2014/mar/14/nasa-civilisation-irreversible-collapse-study-scientists.

137 Keith Kloor, "Judging the Merits of a Media-Hyped 'Collapse' Study," Collide-a-Scape, *Discover* magazine, March 21, 2014, http://blogs.discovermagazine.com/collideascape/2014/03/21/judging-merits-media-hyped-collapse-study.

138 J. Richard Gott III, "Implications of the Copernican Principle for our Future Prospects," *Nature*, vol. 363, pp. 315–19 (1993).

139 John Maynard Keynes, *A Treatise on Probability,* Macmillan and Co., pp. 41–64. (1921).

140 Martin Gardner, "Mathematical Games," Scientific American, Dec. 1970, p. 111.

141 Bradley Morton & Brian Kierland, "How to predict future duration from present age," *The Philosophical Quarterly,* Vol 56, #222, pp. 16–38.

142 John Leslie, "Doomsday Revisited," *Philosophical Quarterly,* vol. 42, pp. 85–7 (1992).

143 Nick Bostrom, 'The Doomsday Argument, Adam & Eve, UN++, and Quantum Joe," Synthese, v.127, pp. 359–87 (2001).

144 P. Buch, "Future prospects discussed," *Nature* v. 368, pp. 107–8.

145 S. Goodman, "Future prospects discussed," *Nature* v. 368, pp. 106–7.

146 J. Richard Gott III, "Our future in the universe" in *Clusters, Lensing, and the Future of the Universe* in *Astronomical Society of the Pacific Conference Series*, v.88, San Francisco, 1996.

147 Elliott Sober, "A Critique of Two Versions of the Doomsday Argument – Gott's Line and Leslie's Wedge," *Synthese*, v. 135, pp. 415–30 (2003).

148 J. R. Baldwin, *et al*, "Failure rates for new Canadian firms," *Statistics Canada*, Minister of industry, catalog #61-526 (2000).

149 Zipf's law, Wikipedia.

150 Gail Tverberg, "World Energy Consumption since 1820 in Charts, *Our Finite World*," http://ourfiniteworld.com/2012/03/12/world-energy-consumption-since-1820-in-charts.

151 Jeff Harding, "The Daily Capitalist: Worldwide Energy Consumption Declines," http://www.noozhawk.com/article/071909_the_daily_capitalist_worldwide_energy_consumption_declines.

152 Notation in *AW* puts $M = (X - X_0)$, which is not used here.

153 Moore's Law, Wikipedia.

154 Quantum Computer, Wikipedia.

155 This is an "obsolete" Wikipedia page; I thought the graph's removal unjustified: http://en.wikipedia.org/w/index.php?title=Moore%27s_law&oldid=618122615.

156 Supercomputer, Wikipedia, Section 1, history.

157 History of Supercomputing, Wikipedia.

158 Sharon Bertsch McGrayne, *The theory that would not die*, Yale U. Press, 2011.

159 Extinction Event, Wikipedia; Section 1, Major extinction events.

160 The Gambler (song), Wikipedia.

161 International Space Station, Wikipedia.

162 United States Department of Defense, Wikipedia.

163 Rule of Succession, Wikipedia.

164 Peter Haggstrom, "Laplace's Law of Succession," http://www.biostat.umn.edu/~dipankar/pubh7440/sunrise.pdf.

165 J. P. Wearing, *The London Stage 1890–1899: A Calendar of Plays and Players*, The Scarecrow Press, Metuchen, NJ & London, 1976. Six more volumes followed, one for each decade, the last being 1950–1959, Scarecrow Press, 1993.

INDEX

Made in the USA
Columbia, SC
23 May 2017